WITHIN LIVING MEMORY

*Recollections of
Old Headington, Oxford*

WITHIN LIVING MEMORY

*Recollections of
Old Headington, Oxford*

COMPILED BY
LESLIE AND GRISELDA TAYLOR

PUBLISHED BY
The Friends of Old Headington
1978

In the event of difficulty in obtaining
this book from a bookshop, orders
may be sent with remittance to
THE FRIENDS OF OLD HEADINGTON
St Andrew's Parish Hall, Dunstan Road
Old Headington, Oxford

©1978 Leslie and Griselda Taylor

ISBN 0 9506065 0 2

Printed in Great Britain at the Alden Press, Oxford

CONTENTS

ACKNOWLEDGEMENTS	*page* 6
FOREWORD	7
INTRODUCTION	8

PART 1: *Village history*

Earliest Headington	9
The Parish Church	9
Houses	20
Public Houses	31
'The British Workman'	33
Schools	35
Women's Institutes	41
Farms and Farming	43
Shops	45
Expansion and Conservation	46

PART 2: *Village memories*

Mr Bert Edney	50
Mrs Edney, Senior	50
Mrs Iris Masters	54
Mr Jack Stow	57
Mrs Coggins	60
Miss Gertie Hedges, Miss Sylvia Parker and Mrs Edie Dickinson	61
Miss Maggie Taylor	63
Mr Bill Berry and Mr Ken Berry	64
Professor E.G.T. Liddell and Mrs Liddell	69
Mrs Horscroft	70
Mrs Corby	71
Miss Katharine Woods	72

ACKNOWLEDGEMENTS

In the compilation of this book over several years we have been helped by so many people willing to give us information of all kinds that it is almost inevitable that we are going to omit some names, and for that we apologize in advance.

At the start we recorded memories on tape, as suggested by the Friends of Old Headington, and here we met with much enthusiasm. The following people, in the order we saw them, were most co-operative and gave us much time: Mr. W.E. Berry, Mrs. Masters, Mrs. D. Coggins, Mrs. Edney Sr, Mr. Jack Stow, Mrs. Dickinson, Miss Sylvia Parker, Miss Gertie Hedges, Professor and Mrs. Liddell, Mr. K.H. Berry, Mr. George Stace and Miss Margaret Stace, Dr. A.B. Emden, Mrs. C.A. Horscroft, Miss Maggie Taylor, Mrs. Corby, Miss Katharine Woods and Miss Margaret Hamersley. To several of these we have had to return as the book grew and new items emerged, for clarification or confirmation, and always we have met with the same eagerness to help. Regrettably some of these good friends have died in the intervening period but we remember them with thanks and admiration.

This material then had to be typed, which presented a major problem. No professional agency was willing to undertake the job. The situation was saved by Miss Mary Kennedy who went through the often blurred tapes word by word and typed them out, a task which took weeks of concentrated work. She then typed our first working draft. We cannot thank her enough for this labour of love.

As we worked on the typescript of memories we saw the need for other sections dealing with Schools, Public Houses, Farming, Shops, etc., if for no other reason than to give colour and setting to the memories. And this brought in more people who verbally answered our many questions. So in addition we want to thank: Mr. and Mrs. Gerald Bale, Mr. John Berry and Miss Muriel Berry, Mr. Leonard Bowles, Mr. Dick Brown, Mr. Percy Cooper, Mr. and Mrs. J.D. Davies, Mr. Dennis (London Road), Mr. Alan Edney, Mr. and Mrs. Fred Edwards, Mr. Harvey Harries (Viking Sports), Mr. H. Hathaway, Mr. Maurice Jacobs, Rev. R.M.C. Jeffery, Miss Levett, and Mrs. Margaret Tite.

We are also indebted to the following for permission to reproduce photographs from their personal collections; Mr. K.H. Berry, Miss Muriel Berry, Mr. W.E. Berry, Mrs. D. Coggins, Mr. and Mrs. J.A. Davies, Mr. A.C. Dring, Mr. Alan Edney, Mr D.S. Frith, Mr. H. Hathaway, Mr. Ian Heggie, Mr. Frank Ricketts, and the Friends of Old Headington.

L.W.T. and E.G.T.

FOREWORD

BY LADY BERLIN

Old Headington is an exceptionally attractive village. Although it has changed greatly since many of the early photographs in this book were taken, it is happily still recognisable. Important village features like the stone garden walls, mostly of random rubble, still remain, as do the stone kerbstones, the pitched roofs covered in slate or tile, and the distinctive terraced cottages. The trees, though sadly decimated by Dutch Elm disease and the recent drought, also remain as a fitting backdrop to buildings made on a human scale.

Although the village is now a Conservation Area, it is subject to all the pressures of a modern urban society. It is plagued by traffic, by pressures to develop large new housing estates, by an accumulation of tasteless minor infilling and addition, and by physical erosion associated with the inexorable passage of time. The latter is particularly worrying because the means—both financial and otherwise—to carry out long-term maintenance and repair is becoming more difficult with each passing year.

The Friends of Old Headington, who encouraged the preparation of this book, have played a vital role in helping to protect and enhance the village. Without their vigilance and foresight the village would surely have succumbed to modern urban pressures. They prevented the speculative development of what is now 'William Orchard Close' by raising loans to buy the site and instigated the preparation of a more suitable scheme; they were the first Oxford amenity society to employ consultants to devise a scheme for the electrification of the old Winsor street lamps, thus preventing their wholesale removal; they were also the first in putting forward concrete proposals for the revision of the adjacent Green Belt, following a village planning study by Buchanan. More recently they have been concerned with stone walls and have done a great deal to encourage, and actually to carry out, repairs to these particularly important features.

But what of the future? This book, which records the life of the village within living memory, shows what a precious thing the residents and local authority hold in trust. We must not, either through complacency or otherwise, betray that trust. The village fabric—both physical and social—can be all too easily destroyed. It goes without saying that it cannot easily be rebuilt.

Headington House, Old Headington ALINE BERLIN
December 1977 President, The Friends of Old Headington

Stoke Place, drawn by Rosemarie Deepwell

INTRODUCTION

There is an old saying that 'down in Oxford the air's like stale, flat beer; up in Headington it's pure champagne'. Perhaps this is one of the reasons why so many people in Headington live to a ripe old age, and many memories go back to well before the twentieth century. So it was felt that it was worth recording the memories of some of these elderly people before modern 'progress' wiped the slate clean. The Friends of Old Headington were anxious that something of this kind should be attempted and a few people were asked to explore possibilities. So a number were interviewed, some tapes were made, copious notes were taken, the main span of which was the last hundred years. Memories are not infallible, and some of the facts given by different people do not always tally. But an effort has been made to check dates and information as much as possible.

A difficulty has been to find some pattern for the whole to provide continuity and interesting reading without too much overlap. The *Victoria County History* gives the complete official history and the main purpose of this little book is to relate personal memories. But it seems appropriate to have a short introductory statement here about early years as a background for what follows.

PART I: VILLAGE HISTORY

EARLIEST HEADINGTON

The earliest known mention of the royal village of Headington is in a deed of Ethelred the Unready, dated the octave of the feast of St. Andrew, the Apostle, (7 December) 1004, recording his gift of its tithes to St. Frideswide's Priory. At that time it was called 'Hedyndon'—the down of Hedde's people—referring to the high shoulder of land on which it is set, overlooking the junction of the Cherwell and the Thames. In the Domesday Book it is called 'Hedintone', but the older version of the name persisted into the fourteenth century.

Headington enters history as the centre of a large royal domain where probably a Mercian Kinglet resided. 'There can be little doubt', wrote Sir Frank Stenton, the eminent medieval historian, 'that when St. Frideswide founded her church, the nearest centre of government was the royal village of Headington from which her successors were receiving the tithes in the last years of the tenth century.' It is likely enough that St. Frideswide herself spent her girlhood in the royal hall here and worshipped in the original timber-built church, before she founded her nunnery by the banks of the Thames in the valley below.

By 912 there had been carved out of the royal domain of Headington a fortified borough, named Oxford, to defend an important passage of the Thames against the Danes and to provide a safe centre for a market. But Headington on its hill continued to be a seat of royalty during the reigns of the later Anglo-Saxon kings. According to tradition King Ethelred was christened here. Henry I (died 1135) was probably the last English King to reside at Headington. As evidence of its former royal connexions Headington continued to be regarded ecclesiastically as a royal peculiar, exempt from the jurisdiction of the Bishops of Lincoln in whose diocese it was before the Reformation*.

THE PARISH CHURCH

The church is the best documented of the buildings in the area and a brief history is given here with more relevant background to the period covered by the people's memories later in this book.

The present building must have had a predecessor, probably a small Saxon building on the same site. The church we now see was established by Hugh de Pluggenait, Lord of the Manor from 1142. The Norman Arch and part of the Chancel date from this time. The

---

* These three paragraphs are taken from the booklet on St. Andrew's Church, Headington, Oxford, prepared with the help of Dr. A.B. Emden, and available from the Vicar.

Church was enlarged with the building of the Lady Chapel through the gift of Philippa, Countess of Warwick. The endowment of the parish was described at that time in the following terms:

'The vicarage (endowment) of the chapelry of Hedindon which belongs to the said Prior and convent of St. Frideswide, as ordained by the authority of the council, consist in all the offerings of the altar, with the small tithes of the whole parish—except the tithe of lambs and the tithe of cheese accruing from the estate of the Lord of the Manor which the Prior and Canon reserved for themselves. Moreover the Vicar shall have the house and freehold in which the Chaplain was wont to reside.'

The church was situated near the road between Dorchester and Oxford and may have been a stopping place for travellers. This could explain the seven-foot high painting of St. Christopher and the mural of the flight into Egypt which once stood on the wall of the Lady Chapel. Over the centuries Vicar succeeded Vicar (see page 14) but they were often absentee vicars and the church was in a poor state. This is well seen in the reply to the Bishop's Visitation in the eighteenth century:

1. The extent of ye parish of Headington is from East to West about sixteen furlongs, from North to South about fourteen furlongs; has two hamlets belonging to it, called Barton and Quarry; there are in ye parish about seventy five families.
2. There are no Papists in ye Parish.
3. There are no Presbyterians, Independents, or AnaBaptists in ye Parish.
4. There are no Quakers in ye Parish.
5. There are no Persons in ye Parish who profess to disregard religion, or that commonly absent themselves from Church.
6. I do not reside, but was excused from it by the late Bishop, because ye Vicarage is not, by itself, good enough to support its Vicar. I take care to have it regularly served and do allow my curate two thirds of ye income; he is not licensed nor did ye late Bishop ever insist upon his taking out a licence because ye vicarage is too small to bear any burthens, expecially as Colleges are such flux bodies, which obliges me to change my curate often; he serves no other cure.
7. Service is duly performed every Sunday and one Sermon preached. Prayers have been read on the 5th day of November, ye 30th of January and ye 29th of May. Children are catechised in Lent and Parents and their children; the catechize has been no otherwise expounded than by preaching. The Sacrament is administered three times in ye year, and usually about twenty receive it.
8. There is neither Free School nor Alms-house in ye Parish.
9. There is no Charity School in ye Parish.
10. No lands or money given to the Church or poor.
11. No Money given at ye Sacrament.
12. Nor is there any other matter relating to ye Parish (that I know of) of which it may be proper to give your Lordship information.

       witness by hand George Bowditch (Vicar 1727–44).

(Note 'vicarage' in this passage refers to the endowment income not to the house—there was none until 1882.)

New life came to the parish under the ministry of the Rev. J.C. Pring, Vicar from 1835 to 1876, although the parish magazine of this period gives us the following critical snippet:

'In 1862 Bishop Wilberforce thought that St. Andrew's was the church in worst repair in the whole of his diocese.'

This comment may have had some effect, as it was during the later years of Mr. Pring's ministry that restoration of the church was begun and also some extension of church life in the district. This may have been due largely to his curate, Rev. L.S. Tuckwell.

In 1864, the architect, Mr. J.C. Buckler, had extended the nave westward, at a cost of £3,000. By 1869 the curate was apparently receiving contributions which he proposed to employ in the erection of the North Aisle, the cost of which was estimated at £1,000. £400 would be contributed by two Church Building Societies, £200 to be collected by the curate; and by April 1869, £400 had still to be contributed before the proposed restoration would be undertaken. By December 1870 the North Aisle Fund had reached £460.0.6. The builder's contract for the aisle was £794.7.6; the contract for the sittings, if of deal £170, or if of oak, about £450. Additional expenses including fees of the architects and clerk of the works were estimated at £200, thus the cost of the work as far as was then ascertained was about £1,200. It was hoped to begin building in the spring of 1871. In September 1875 there was an appeal to finish work on the north aisle. Towards the original appeal for £1,000 only £605.18.0 had been raised. In 1881, the north aisle, with porch and vestry had been completed.

One interesting footnote—In 1878 it was reported that 14 choirmen had drunk 5 gallons of best beer at their annual Christmas supper. They had also ordered a bottle of gin and one of whisky, but the Vicar refused to pay for these. The result was that seven of the choir walked out.

In the *Headington Parish Magazine* for June 1870 there is the following extract: 'It is proposed to build a small brick Church in the district of New Headington for the benefit chiefly of that part of our parish. A piece of ground has been obtained and it is hoped that before long the building will be commenced. The cost of the building and land will not be less than £300. Donations amounted to £105 have been promised.' And in the September number we read:

'The Little Church in New Headington is now progressing rapidly. It will be ready for service we hope before the 1st November. Mr. Joseph Castle of Oxford is the builder. The cost of the building will be about £250; the necessary fittings may be estimated at £50; and the purchase of the ground together with the erection of a boundary wall will bring the total expenditure up to £350.' Contributions at that time amounted to £119.8.0 but by the end of November this had risen to £167.14.0, with £150 still wanted.

The Chapel was opened for Divine Service on Thursday, 3 November 1870, with the Lord Bishop of Oxford, John Mackarness, preaching at morning service at 11 a.m. and the Rev. Dr. William Bright of Christ Church preaching at 7 p.m. 70 persons attended Morning Prayer and Holy Communion and their offertory amounted to £21.11.0.

A church was built in Headington Quarry to counter the strong Methodist influence there in 1849.

The Rev. E.F.G. Tyndale, appointed in 1879, developed a High Church tradition in the parish. He was succeeded in 1889 by the Rev. Holford Scott who later changed his name to Scott-Tucker. He was a teetotaller and encouraged abstinence in the parish. (See 'The

St. Andrew's choir in Father Townson's time. Mr. George Stace, Sr. in back row.

British Workman, p. 33) It was in his time that the schools began to be established. (See p. 36).

There were usually several curates at this time. When Mr. Scott-Tucker left in 1899, the brother of one of the then curates became the Vicar. He was the Rev. F.C. Townson, whose ministry in Old Headington was unforgettable. Father Townson was an extreme Anglo-Catholic of a very militant sort. He raised the churchmanship to unknown levels and alienated most of the congregation in the process. He also came into conflict with the Bishop of Oxford. The end of the story was tragic, because he clearly became a mentally-sick man and had to be suspended. He left the parish in 1917.

It was because of this period in the life of the Church that many of the church-goers left St. Andrew's and went off to the chapel in New Headington and there helped to build up the life of the now separate parish of All Saints', Highfield.

The next vicar was the Rev. A.N. Armstrong whose task was to put the parish on a more even keel. His work was therefore slow and quiet. In 1924 he was succeeded by the Rev. Henry Edward Bird. 'Dicky Bird' as he was known remained as Vicar until 1946. There are many people who remember him as a rather quiet and dry clergyman who sustained a regular level of ministry over a long time. He was ably supported by his younger and very active wife, who was deeply involved in the life of the village. Mr. Bird was much interested in the history of St. Andrew's and much of the earlier material given in this section is the result of researches which he carried out.

In 1961 the chancel was repaved and the altar brought forward; and a baptistry was formed in the space under the tower by transferring the font from the north-west corner of the nave.

Two more bells were added to the existing six in 1975.

Now in 1977 there has been a Church Restoration Appeal over several months and a Headington Festival to meet expenses for major repairs to the roof, masonry, lighting and flooring as well as possible resiting of the seating. So in the future the church may look different from what it does today.

Windows in the Church

There are some windows in the church which deserve mention.

1. The east window of the Chancel Chapel depicting the Adoration of the Magi, was designed by Henry Holiday and erected in 1891. It has the following inscription—

'To the Glory of God and in loving memory of Edmund Francis Guise Tyndale, M.A. Magdalen College Oxford for 10 years (1879–1889) the devoted Vicar of Headington this window is erected by his many friends. Easter 1891'

2. On the north wall of the Chancel there is a window inscribed as follows—

'Saint Thomas Aquinas To the greater Glory of God. In memory of Christian Steenbuck. Priest, born November 7 1876 & died December 1st 1926 who celebrated at this altar. May he rest in peace'

The Rev. Christian Steenbuck was assisting in the parish at that time. It is unusual in an Anglican Church to find a widow depicting Saint Thomas Aquinas.

'To the Glory of God and in affectionate remembrance of the Rev. John Robinson who died November 22 1864 of small-pox contracted in the discharge of his duties as curate of this Parish. By Public Subscription AD 1865'

3. The south windows in the Chancel, designed by H.C. Murray, London, depict S. Margaret tending sheep and S. Margaret and the Dragon.

4. The east window of the Lady Chapel has the inscription—

5. The south windows of the Lady Chapel were offered by A. Wylie 1884 and W.M. Wylie 1884 (See p. 28).

6. The 'unique' west window.

It may be wondered why this window has been referred to as 'unique'. This excellent example of modern stained glass, designed by Archibald Nicholson, commemorates Vashti de Montfort Wellbourne. On one side of the window is a vigorous figure of Simon de Montfort on horseback bearing the inscription 'Founder of the English Parliament' and on the other side a stately crowned figure of the sitting Queen with a life-like panther at her feet with the inscription 'Vashti, Queen of Persia'. Below is a pictorial representation of Barton Manor and of the Chapter House at Westminster.

The Rev. George Day, Vicar of St. Andrew's, talking to Mr. S.P.B. Mais for an article in the *Oxford Mail* in January 1955, said 'I don't suppose there is another window to Vashti in the country, and there was some difficulty in getting the Chancellor to allow this one. He at first refused, but when it was ingeniously pointed out to him that Queen Vashti was most virtuous and exemplary in her refusal to attend her husband in his cups the Chancellor allowed it to be put up'.

When the organ built by J.W. Walker and Sons for Merton College was to be put into St. Andrew's Church, in 1967, it was found that the only place for it was in front of the west window. So it was decided to inform the Wellbourne family, who had given the west window some years before, that this was likely to happen. Mr. Graham Pollard, then living at Barton Manor, 7 Barton Village Road, wrote in reply in August 1967:

'I know little for certain and doubt whether anyone of the Wellbourne family now survives. The story I have heard, is that a lady whose maiden name I do not know, about 1870 married a barrister called Wellbourne. He died about 1873, leaving his widow unprovided for, and an infant daughter, Vashti de Montfort Wellbourne. The widow shortly afterwards married as her second husband an eminent pork butcher called Hedges in Oxford. He died I believe before 1900. . . . Mr. Hedges bought Barton Manor, when he married, from a man called Jennings who was a wood engraver who worked with Orlando Jewitt. Vashti de Montfort Wellbourne became an actress in Sir Ben Greet's Shakespearean company. She ran the Barton Academy of Dramatic Art, and started the first cinema in Oxford in Walton Street about 1910. She died of cancer under the cherry tree in what is now my garden, in 1930. This is the right hand tree nearest the house below Vashti, Queen of Persia, in your west window. . . . Mrs. Hedges died in 1937 and left Barton Manor to a Mr. Pether of Stowford Farm who was her or her husband's nephew. Mr. Pether died about 1946 and left Barton Manor to a Miss Iris Munro who was manageress of the Golden Cross in the Cornmarket, She died about 1948 and left it to her nephew who sold it to Hall's Brewery. . . . I am sorry that the picture of the house where I live, in your west window, is to be covered up.'

Left: St. Andrew's Norman Arch. *Right:* The Fish window.

As a more recent addition there is the 'Fish' window in the Baptistry. This commemorates the inauguration of the Fish Good Neighbour Scheme in the parish in 1961. It was given by one of the co-founders of the Fish movement, which has now spread to several thousand areas in the United Kingdom and throughout the world, particularly in the United States of America.

Vicars of St. Andrew's, Headington

A list of Vicars and Curates-in-Charge from about 1000, many of whom were non-resident, is shown on a record board in the church. The following is the list from 1804.

	Instituted	Patron
Rev. Thomas Henry Whorwood	1804	Henry Mayne Whorwood
Rev. Joseph Charles Pring	1835	Rev. Thomas Henry Whorwood
Rev. Alleyn Ward Pearson	1876	Rev. Thomas Henry Whorwood
Rev. Edmund Frances Guise Tyndale	1879	Rev. Thomas Henry Whorwood
Rev. John Holford Scott (Scott-Tucker later)	1889	Mr. and Mrs. Ralph Rawlinson.
Rev. Robert Walter Townson	1899	Mr. and Mrs. Ralph Rawlinson
Rev. Alexander Nenon Armstrong	1916	Mr. and Mrs. Ralph Rawlinson
Rev. Henry Edward Bird	1924	Mrs. Rawlinson / Keble College (1924)
Rev. George Edmund Day	1946	Keble College
Rev. Derek Ian Tennant Eastman	1956	Keble College
Rev. Christopher Robin Paul Anstey	1964	Keble College
Rev. Robert Martin Colquhoun Jeffery	1971	Keble College

Some details from Parish Magazines, 1869–1900

Some more interesting facts of local history emerged from the Parish magazines.

In 1868 church collections amounted to £65.19.8¼ of which £28.5.8 went for the relief of the poor, £14.6.6 for church restoration, £9.19.9¼ for the maintenance of the Sunday Evening Services, £4.11.0 for the parish schools, £4.18.0 for the Radcliffe Infirmary, and £3.18.9 for the Diocesan Church Building Society. Collections were made once a month in the church to pay off the debt incurred in restoration work.

The *Headington Parish Magazine*, edited in 1869 and 1870 by the curate, the Rev. L.S. Tuckwell, invited communications to the Editor. These had to be left at the Post Office, the corner shop in Old High Street, at that date run by Mr. Rance, and later by the Rudds (see p. 45). The cost of the magazine was 1½d, or, if distributed by the District Visitors, 1d. But in spite of this, the magazine had a deficit of £5.9.5¼ over the year 1869, although they seem to have sold 294 copies at 1½d, 2,103 at 1d. and 285 'outsides' at ½d. In 1871 magazine sales were 208 at 1½d or 1d. and the deficit was down to seven shillings.

The curate in 1869 was the Rev. L.S. Tuckwell, who was a splendid musician. He lived for some time at the Hermitage, and gave several concerts a year for different good causes.

The same magazine gives us a general picture of the village, which included New Headington and Barton at that date. There were a number of Headington Parish Charities, such as the clothing club, the coal club, the lying-in society, and the benevolent society. In June 1869 the parish started a district visiting society, and this gives us a very interesting list of the number of houses and inhabitants in the various streets. In High Street, now Old High Street, there were 60 houses and they contained 222 inhabitants. In Church Lane, now St. Andrew's Lane, there were 24 houses, with 93 inhabitants. In Church Street, now St. Andrew's Road, there were 28 houses with 122 inhabitants.

There seem to have been a number of general holidays. On the Tuesday in Whitsun week for instance, the village celebrated a general holiday. People assembled at 11 o'clock in the morning, went to morning service, and then walked in procession round the village, preceded by a band playing a number of popular tunes. At 2 o'clock they sat down to dinner at the Britannia Inn, and afterwards in an adjoining field they played sports and games in which everyone joined. Another holiday was the Harvest Festival. Then they had sports and games in the Manor grounds belonging to Mr. Watson-Taylor. The grounds opened at 2.30 p.m. and closed at 7 p.m. and tickets of admission were 2d each. Tickets to admit to the ground and the tea were 8d each, and Mr. Wyatt of the White Hart provided the tea. Annual Harvest Thanksgiving Festivals are mentioned several times. In 1871 one was held on 14 September and was thought to be the most successful that had ever been held. 'The festivities began with Morning Prayer and Sermon at 11 a.m. and ended with Evensong and Sermon at 7.30 p.m. At 1 p.m. the visitors were entertained to luncheon in the garden of Linden House, (now the Priory) which Mr. Franklin kindly lent for the occasion. At 2 p.m. Mr. Watson-Taylor's grounds were thrown open to all the parishioners and their friends. As many as 1,100 assembled and enjoyed sports, music, and dancing until 7 p.m.'

In 1871 the village had a population of 1,536 and a registered record of 53 baptisms, 5 marriages, and 18 burials.

An advertisement appeared at that time for a house wanted by Mr. Vallis, the headmaster of the Field Schools, containing two sitting rooms and three bedrooms, with a piece of garden attached, annual rent to be not more than £14 or £15. In the same year there was an advertisement from Rance, tea, grocery and general stores in High Street, now Old High Street. He advertised his best non-explosive oil with the least possible smell for burning in paraffin lamps for 3 shillings a gallon.

A Headington and Oxford carrier, George Gardiner of the Anchor Inn, Cornmarket, advertised in 1870 that he started from Headington on Mondays and Saturdays at 8 a.m. and 2 p.m. On other days, Sundays excepted, at 11 a.m. only. Caroline Taylor, living near the church, advertised her willingness to take in a family's washing on moderate terms.

On Monday in Whitsun week, 29 May 1871, the first stone of an institution, to be called the Wingfield Convalescent Home, was laid on a site within the parish by the Venerable Archdeacon Clerke. Mrs. Wingfield, 'long known and, we are confident, long to be remembered in Oxford for the good works and alms-deeds which she did', was the main contributor to the undertaking; about one half of the sum raised by its promoters having been given by her, and hence its designation. 'The Wingfield Convalescent Home, capable of enlargement under the plan most kindly given by the architect, Mr. William Wilkinson, will accommodate only 8 patients at a time; but as their residence will be limited to what is necessary, it is calculated that a large number may actually be received within its walls.' It was opened in May 1872, when a report in the June number of the *Headington Magazine* reminds its readers that 'this Institution is intended for persons who are cured, but still weak, and in need of rest, good air, and wholesome food. Many a man and woman, after leaving hospital, is still unable to do a day's work; this Home provides persons with what they require in this way, who may be sent hither by the Physician or Surgeon of the Radcliffe Infirmary.'

In 1872 the Harvest Festival was again the big social occasion of the year. The athletic sports were conducted by Mr. Montague Wootten—'cricket and football, with various games set on foot for the amusement of the girls.' The writer of this description completes the picture by adding 'the happy countenance of the more aged bore testimony to their enjoyment of this holiday gathering: Mr. Loder, with his photographic apparatus, was present to take the portraits of all who had the patience to "sit" for him; and the band of the Oxfordshire Militia, stationed in the middle of the grounds, gladdened and cheered the hearts of all around. At 3.30 p.m. a large tent was thrown open, and about 400 persons partook of an excellent tea, supplied by Mr. Wyatt of the White Hart, after which dancing began and was kept up until 7 o'clock.'

This is the first mention of the Wootten family, who occupied Headington House and White Lodge (see p. 20).

In 1873 there were 36 burials (20 men and 16 female, the average age at death being 40½ years).

In August 1881 the first flower show in the grounds of the Manor House was held and was a great success. This was to be held annually for many years to come.

In the same year, negotiations with Mr. R. Godfrey for the purchase of St. Andrew's House (see p. 26) as a vicarage were completed. Money for this had been raised during the previous year or so and the Vicar, the Rev. E.F.G. Tyndale, moved in early in 1882. Prior to this date Vicars seem to have had no fixed abode in the parish.

The new cemetery site was purchased in 1884, consecrated in January 1885, and the first interment there, of Mr. James Rogers, aged 70, took place in September of that year.

In 1889 the Headington Amateur Choral and Dramatic Society was started. This, over the years, became a very flourishing and popular activity, and many villagers of all kinds took part in it. The performances were at first given in the British Workman.

In 1890 we read that 'the iron room' was being erected, 'which should be useful for meetings in this part of the parish'. This was originally put up in Barton and later removed by Mr. Townson to the Vicarage garden, where it was used extensively until the new Parish Hall was opened in 1958.

In the same year we are told that half a dozen new houses had been built and that the New Headington roads had been put into decent order. In the 1891 Census, there were 466 inhabited houses, 36 uninhabited ones, and 5 were being built. This presumably includes New Headington as well as Old Headington. The population consisted of 1,011 males and 1,145 females.

In 1891 also the idea was put forward for lighting the village by oil lamps. Money was collected for 4 standard lamps. The Bullingdon Highway Board approved them but laid down various conditions. Then comes silence and it is not sure what happened.

In 1892 the Headington branch of the Oxford Co-operative Society was opened on Easter Monday. This was in London Road and for many years was the one big shop of the area. We are also told that during this year there were at least 40 stonemasons living in the parish and even more carpenters, joiners, and possibly bricklayers. It was on account of these building workers that Mr. Charles Ricketts recommended that a course of geometrical drawing would be useful. This was undertaken by Mr. Stace at the Boys School twice a week, supported by the Oxfordshire County Council Technical Education Committee.

In 1893 the Football Club was started by Dr. Hitchings, who had married the year before and had settled in his house in London Road, where Fine Fare now stands. The Cricket Club had been active for some years before.

It was in December 1894, as a result of the Local Government Act of that year, that Headington elected its first Parish Council of 15 members. Mr. Montague Wootten was the first chairman. They dealt with all kinds of local matters—such as allotments, footpaths, the recreation ground, etc. (See note below.) This winter was very cold and 'Free breakfasts were given to many of the children attending our schools'. Influenza raged and many were struck down. Perhaps here it is worth mentioning that the Havelock Lodge of Oddfellows, so often mentioned in the memories, acted as a kind of insurance, like Friendly Societies, against illness and death. Members paid in regular subscriptions and were helped when in need. In 1895 the Headington Nursing Association was started. For the first two years a nurse from the Acland Nursing Home came to live at the Wingfield Convalescent Home for the winter and early spring, and was on call in Headington, Quarry, Barton and New Marston as a district nurse. She charged one penny a visit or four pence a week. In 1897 enough money had been raised for the nurse to be able to live in Headington the whole year round. And a bicycle was bought for her.

* * *

Further information about parish administration has been obtained from Mr. Leonard Bowles, who, after working under William Coppock, became Assistant Overseer of the Headington Parish Council (incorporating the areas of Quarry, Highfield and Old Headington) in April 1924. This was a paid post and carried with it the duties of Clerk to the Parish Council; the work was concerned with valuations, rents, etc. Three part-time overseers, elected annually, helped him. These elections caused fierce controversy, at times ending in fighting with staves in the old Manor Road. Among the chairmen of the Parish Council were Dr. Massie of Charlton Lea (later the Rookery) and Mr. Franklin, the

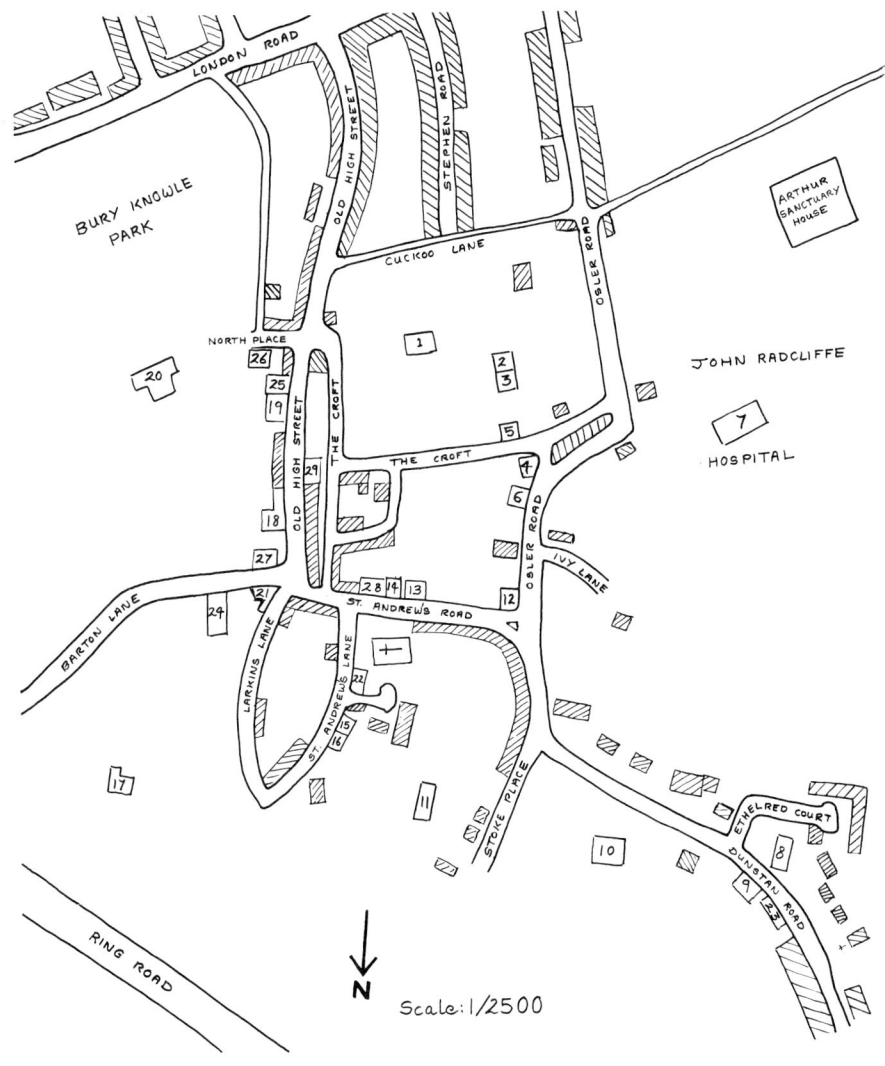

1. Headington House
2. White Lodge
3. Sandy Lodge
4. The Court
5. Waldencote
6. The Old Pound House
7. The Manor House
8. Manor Farm House
9. West Lodge
10. The Rookery (Ruskin Hall)
11. Stoke
12. St. Andrew's House
13. Laurel Farm
14. Church House
15. Unity House
16. North Lodge
17. The Grange
18. The Priory
19. The Hermitage
20. Bury Knowle
21. Mathers Farm
22. Church Hill Farm
23. Lower Farm
24. The Barn
25. 'The British Workman'
26. Old Infants School
27. The Black Boy
28. The White Hart
29. The Bell

Map of the Village, 1978

coroner. The minute book of the Overseers of Headington Parish from about 1810 to 1929 is now in the Bodleian Library.

In April 1927 the Parish Council became known as the Urban District Council of Headington and had its office at the corner of Stile Road and London Road. In 1929 it was incorporated into the City of Oxford. It was then that Mr. Bowles decided to set up on his own as an estate agent in Windmill Road.

HOUSES

Headington House

Owned, at least as far back as 1869, by the merchant banking family of Wootten Wootten, Headington House is frequently referred to in the Memories. Its adjoining park and fields stretched to the London Road, with Old High Street on one side and Osler Road (then called Sandy Lane) on the other. Mrs. Edney, Senior, remembered it as 'a park with chestnut trees round up to the London Road, and aconites and snowdrops in the first part of the drive'. There were two lodges to the House, one in London Road, mentioned by Mrs. Horscroft (see p. 70), and one in Osler Road beside Cuckoo Lane. The present lodge in Old High Street was built at the turn of the century. Before that there were evidently some almshouses. The bridges over Cuckoo Lane (then called the Hawthorns) led from the garden to the other parts of the estate. We are told that Cuckoo Lane—a right of way—was sunk so that the people passing along it could not be seen from the House.

William Wootten Wootten died in 1887 and his widow Sarah in 1904. The two remaining unmarried daughters later moved to North Oxford and the house was empty for some time.

The meadows to the south of the House, bordered by Old High Street, London Road and Osler road, on which the Wootten Jersey cows grazed, were let to Mr. Hathaway of Highfield (see p. 44). But gradually after the First World War the whole area was sold off as building plots. Mrs. Masters remembers that the corner where Barclays Bank now stands was offered for £75 by Mr. Hamlet of Hamlet and Dulake. Her father 'thought it was far too much money to pay'. In the end it was bought by Harry Berry the butcher who sold it to Mr. Guy Thomson of Woodperry House, father of Sir John Thomson, late Lord Lieutenant of the County.

In 1912 Mr. A.H. Franklin bought the house, living there until he died in 1932. He was followed by the Stoyes and in 1953 Lady Berlin acquired it.

White Lodge/Sandy Lodge

It was in 1881 that William Wootten Wootten, of Headington House, bought this house and land, which included the one-storey stone-built lodge on Osler Road, then Sandy

Lane. (This has been enlarged, and is now 38 Osler Road.) The big house was much smaller than it is now. When his son, Montague Wootten, married in 1888, William's widow, Sarah, 'devised' the house to him and there he and his family lived until his suicide in 1909.

Monty Wootten, who followed his father's footsteps in the Bank of Wootten, Parsons and Thomson, was a great figure in the village, interested in sport and chairman of the first Parish Council set up in 1894. Mrs. Coggins has happy memories of the garden parties in the early years of this century, when as a child she watched the elegant guests arriving in carriages and pairs.

With Montague Wootten's death, things began to change. From 1909–1914 White Lodge was leased, together with The Court—not yet known by that name—and 6 The Croft, to the Newhams. They were an American family, and employed a retired jockey, Amos Hunt, who also looked after the Vicar's horses. He used to drive the Miss Townsons (the vicar's daughters) in a little pony cart. During the First World War Mr. F.L. Evans took over the lease of White Lodge and it was during those war years that Headington School was started in White Lodge under Miss Mulliner and Miss Porcher.

In 1920 Mr. Edwin J. Hall, a local business man, (see p. 55) bought the whole property from Montague Wootten's executors. The house was then divided into two. In 1921 he sold White Lodge South, now White Lodge, to Walter Smith who lived there for many years. His son, Alec Smith, later became Warden of New College. When his parents died it was rented for a time by Professor Kilner, the plastic surgeon. In 1922 Mr. Hall sold White Lodge North—now Sandy Lodge—to Mr. and Mrs. Holmes. Mrs. Holmes died in 1924 and in 1925 Mr. W.H. Hamersley bought it for his retirement in 1927. After his death in 1941 Mrs. Hamersley stayed on with their daughter Margaret (see p. 40) until 1953, when the Wiles bought it; and in 1963 Sandy Lodge became the property of the Bales.

The Court

The Court, as some of the older inhabitants first remember it, was an ivy-covered stone cottage with a sitting-room, kitchen and three bedrooms. The Miss Wilkins rented it from the Wootten family and ran a small dairy farm there, where one could buy butter and milk. Later the Wootten's coachman, Mr. Hicks, lived there with his family. When the Wootten estate was sold up in 1914 a Miss Gertrude Drage bought the house, together with part of the old village pound. Then Mrs. Dowdenay, a professional singer, is mentioned. Lord Sholto Douglas, a bachelor who called himself 'the last of the Stuarts', altered the house a good deal, adding a little Roman Catholic chapel— now a spare bedroom—raising the front wall and putting in the present wrought-iron gates, making it, in fact, as it is today. He also filled in a cellar which, rumour has it, had been used for strange undergraduate orgies. He was living there during the late twenties. The Snows occupied the house until, in the thirties, they built and moved to Southway in Dunstan Road. During the Second World War the Creswicks owned the house. Mr. Creswick was very fitness-conscious and was a leading light in the local Home Guard. Since 1948 the Turville-Petres have lived there.

Waldencote

Waldencote was bought by Mr. E.J. Hall with White Lodge. It housed the electric generator whose $3\frac{1}{2}$ horse-power oil engine had provided electric light for the house. This part of the estate was sold in 1921 to Ida Christina Mackintosh and was converted into a dwelling house with an internal iron spiral staircase. The first resident who is remembered is Mrs. Cameron, who wrote under the name of Elizabeth Bowen. She was married to Mr. A.C. Cameron, the Chief Education Officer for the City of Oxford. The Parkers lived there for many years before it was sold to Mr. A.A. Williams, Bursar of The Queen's College, to whom it now belongs.

The Old Pound House

The land on which this house lies was sold in 1899 by G.H. Morrell M.P., who then lived at Headington Hill Hall, to Montague Wootten Wootten of White Lodge. It then consisted of coach houses, stables and gardens. In the same year Montague Wootten bought the village pound for £10 from the Lord of the Manor of Headington (i.e. the Peppercorns). The pound was last used in 1875. The village stocks were also there until they were moved to the bottom of Shotover Hill, at the corner of Old Road and Quarry Road.

In 1914 Chaloner T.T. Kemshead bought the land from Montague Wootten's executors—except for half the pound which had been added to the Court property. By this time Oxford City drainage and water supply had been laid on. Adapting the existing out-buildings, Mr. Kemshead built a dwelling house which became known as the Hatch or Hutch. In 1927 the house was sold to J.G. Edwards, Fellow of Jesus College, who lived there until 1949 when, now known as the Old Pound House, it was bought by Magdalen College. The Tites lived there, and in 1966 the present property was conveyed to them.

The Manor House

The Manor House with its Manorial Rights was sold by the Whorwoods in 1849 to William Peppercorn who thus became Lord of the Manor. The House was leased by him to the Watson-Taylors and, when the surviving Miss Watson-Taylor died in 1892, it was rented to Colonel James Hoole who bought it from William Peppercorn in 1906.

There are many memories of the annual Flower Show and sports held in the grounds each August, starting in 1881. Colonel Hoole died in 1917, and the estate was bought by the Radcliffe Infirmary. By 1926 the Osler Pavilion was opened for the City authorities. It accommodated 20 T.B. patients (10 male and 10 female). This was closed in 1969.

Sunnyside was originally a convalescent home administered by the Radcliffe Infirmary.

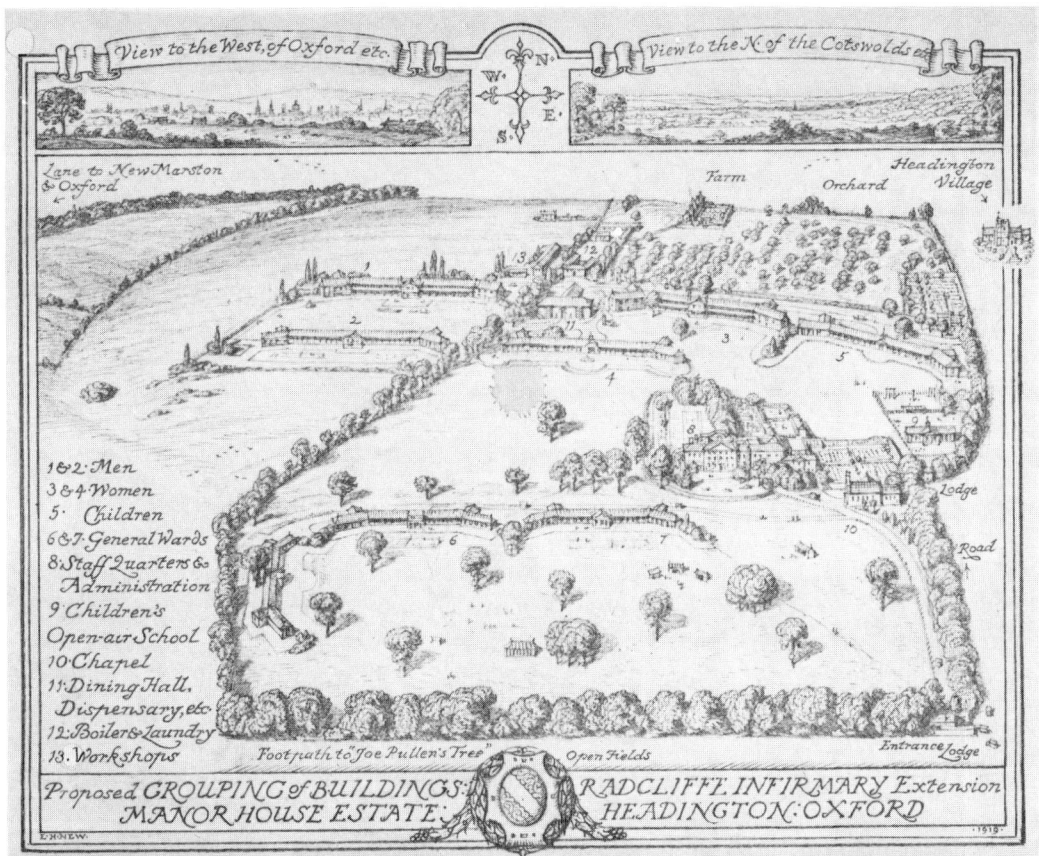

Proposals made in 1919.

After 1954 it was used for T.B. patients and for those with other diseases of the chest. It also was closed in 1969 when plans for the new John Radcliffe Hospital were moving ahead. The open-air school, now the Ormerod School (see p. 41) was set up in 1928. The Manor House itself was used as a nurses' residence until the new Arthur Sanctuary House was built in 1955. Now it houses the offices of the Oxfordshire Area Health Authority (Teaching).

Manor Farm House

This was a working farm house until the twenties (see p. 44) with, we are told, 'a lovely old-world herb garden'. It belonged to the Lords of the Manor (the Peppercorns), but in 1906 Colonel Hoole bought it and reunited it to the Manor grounds. When John Wiggins, the farmer, left, there were several different occupiers, including the Sanctuaries for a time. Dr. Rose Innes, the tuberculosis specialist, finally bought the house. He made many additions to it in the early thirties, including the two wings on the west, but a few years later he himself contracted T.B. and went to South Africa. Then the McGarveys bought the property and when they died the house and grounds were sold and Ethelred Court was built towards the end of the sixties.

West Lodge

West Lodge seems to have always looked much as it does today, save that at one time it had some cottages, now pulled down, along its front wall. Colonel Finch Noyes, who married Kate Wootten, lived there in the 1890s. He was followed by a veterinary surgeon called Joseph Stowe who was there until he died in 1926. It was then that Jack Kingerlee of the building firm bought it, living there until his death in the early sixties, when Dr. D.H. Richards and his family moved in.

The Rookery

The Rookery (now known as Ruskin Hall) was a preparatory school for boys, owned by the Rev. J.W.A. Taylor in the early 1870s and taken over by Dr. Gibson in the early 1880s. He lived there until 1897, when the house went to Captain Price and his two sisters. By 1910 Dr. John Massie had moved in. He was a Doctor of Law and went to London three or four days a week to attend his practice. He renovated the house, then called Charlton Lea, employing 50 Headington workmen. He gravelled the drive and always kept it spick and span. He employed 6 maids in the house and had 12 outdoor staff. He had two cars, one a Daimler for the winter months, and an open-top one for fine weather. His chauffeur lived in the present Osler Road.

Dr. Massie died in 1926, three months after Dick Brown joined his outdoor staff, from whom we get much of this information. Mrs. Massie stayed on until her death in 1933. She took a keen interest in the garden, and Mr. Brown remembers her in her bath-chair, being pushed around by Mr. Dixon the houseman. At that time Mr. Dawes was the head gardener, and lived at what is now 39 St. Andrew's Road, a house built by Dr. Massie specifically for him on the site of Samson Smith's old house (see p. 62). It was called 'Hambledon' and is unchanged today except for additions at the back and a garage built by Mr. John Alden.

When Mrs. Massie died, Colburns, builders from Swindon, bought the house and land for development, but Oxford City Council refused planning permission, and so in November 1933 Sir Michael Sadler bought it. He was a prominent member of the Oxford Preservation Trust and just about to retire from being Master of University College. He also had the pillar box put in the wall just outside his gate, bringing the total of pillar boxes in Old Headington to three. Sir Michael remodelled the garden, adding various sculptures by Henry Moore and Epstein, etc., and had many valuable pictures in the house. He liked to think that it was in the well in the very old walled fruit garden at the back of the house, now the tennis court, that Saint Dunstan baptised King Ethelred, but research refutes this.

After Sir Michael died in 1943, Mr. Gurden, partner in a large bakery and confectionery business, bought the house and grounds. Almost immediately the War Office requisitioned it, and at first 140 American girls were stationed there, sleeping in Nissen huts to the west side of the house. Later it became a convalescent home for Americans until the end of the war. It was restored in 1946 and Mr. Sam Smith rented it for Ruskin College for a year, after which Mr. Gurden offered it for sale—all except the land on which the present Charlton Lea (4 Dunstan Road) was later built—and it became the property of Ruskin College.

Stoke

Stoke belonged to a Mr. Dockray, who married the daughter of the Rev. J.W.A. Taylor, headmaster of the Rookery School. Mr. Dockray was a master at the school, and his wife was an artist who often exhibited at the Royal Academy. She painted portraits of many local people. Mr. Dockray was the People's Warden at St. Andrew's Church for various years between 1888 and 1908.

The next owners were the Melville-Lees, father and son, and they enlarged the house considerably before it was sold to Ruskin College in 1965.

Stoke Cottage, 1, Stoke Place

This is of interest as it was the last house in Old Headington to remain thatched. It was re-roofed in the mid-1960s. For many years the house was occupied by Charlie Morris, the builder, who died in 1931. The builder's yard was behind the house and a right-of-way led to it behind the Rookery cottages in Stoke Place. There is still some conflict over this right of way.

27–33 St. Andrew's Road

There were ten thatched cottages in the old Church Street where the four pink houses now stand. The first cottage stood next to the entrance gate of 35 St. Andrew's Road. Seven of these cottages stood on the pavement (but with long, narrow gardens), and three of them down by the existing church wall. There was one pump which supplied water for them all in a yard at the back, and four earth closets in a row which the tenants took turns to empty in their gardens. By the 1920s cold-water taps had been fitted in the cottages. Mr. Percy Cooper remembers Mr. Harris who did the dyeing and cleaning for the village in great wooden tubs. These cottages were condemned in the late nineteen thirties. Four local inhabitants—John Johnson of Bareacres, Professor E.G.T. Liddell of the Hermitage, Alec Smith, Warden of New College, who owned White Lodge and Dr. A.B. Emden—put up the money to build the present crescent when the cottages were pulled down. The architect was Mr. Fielding Dodd and the new houses were completed in 1939. These houses were handed over to the Oxford Preservation Trust, who charged a shilling a year groundrent on a 999-year lease.

Miss Dakin bought no. 27. She kept some very fine white goats in the Laurel Farm

Stoke Cottage as it was when thatched.

orchard and was often seen walking them out down Dunstan Road. Dr. Richards and family moved in in 1951, and added a surgery behind their garage a year or two later. They were followed by the Bayleys and the Cooks. At no. 29 was Miss Radcliffe, daughter of Judge Radcliffe who used to live on Headington Hill. She died in 1970. No. 31 was bought by Mr. Gould, a master at Wellington College, who wanted it for his retirement. He let the house during the Second World War to Mr. Joseph Tumim, Clerk to the Assizes and in 1944 to the Taylors, who a few years later persuaded Mr. Gould to sell. Canon Demant bought it in 1968 when they moved to Dunstan Road. No. 33 was first bought by Mrs. Mair, later to become the wife of Sir William Beveridge who planned the National Welfare Scheme. Mr. Tumim bought it in 1943 and moved in from next door. He was followed by the Petersons and the McDowells before it was bought by the Church Commissioners as a vicarage in 1977.

St. Andrew's House

In the early nineteenth century the ex-Vicarage consisted of a house and four cottages. The whole site was bought in 1862 by John Mason, Wine Merchant, who pulled down the cottages in order to extend his garden and built the present house, calling it St. Andrew's House. When John Mason's widow died in 1880, the property passed to Robert Godfrey of Birmingham, John Mason's brother-in-law, who conveyed it to Queen Anne's bounty as a parsonage house. The Rev. E.F.G. Tyndale and family moved into it in 1882, and it was the home of our vicars until 1977 when it was sold to Mr. Atkinson, Head of the Planning Department at the Oxford Polytechnic, and 33 St. Andrew's Road became the new vicarage.

Laurel Farm

(See Farms and Farming). Mrs. Tagg lived on in the house until her death in 1969 at the age of 93. Corpus Christi College kept the house itself and a small part of the garden for one of their dons. The orchard and remaining part of the garden was sold in 1975 to the Oxford City Council for housing.

Church House

This was the home of Mrs. Edgcombe, who died in 1896. Some time later Mr. and Mrs. Surman lived there. Her father was a gardener and she went to school with Mrs. Coggins. Then came Mr. and Mrs. Field, he being a retired schoolmaster. In 1923 Sir Charles and Lady Nicholson bought the house, but did not live in it permanently until 1931. Sir Charles was a well-known church architect and the first Lady Nicholson was a Miss Olivier, sister of the owner of 3 St. Andrew's Road.

10 St. Andrew's Road

In the late nineteenth century a Miss Clarke lived here. She played the harmonium and was a very active church worker, helping with the clothing and coal clubs etc. In the late nineties she was clerk to the Parish Council and in 1897 was made Church Warden of St. Andrew's. The morning after Good Friday one year in the early twenties, her maid could not get into her bedroom—which she always locked at night. She sent for Mr. Coggins who brought a ladder to get up to her room to find Miss Clarke had died in her sleep. Mr. and Mrs. Pontin then lived there. Miss Moore followed them, then Dr. and Mrs. Peat for a short while before Mrs. Dupuis bought it.

1 St. Andrew's Lane

This consisted originally of two cottages. It was bought at the turn of the century by the elderly Miss Macaulay, Lord Macaulay's sister. In 1910 William Mattock, Mrs. Masters' father, bought it for £150 and moved there with his young family from Barton. In 1953 the Housemans bought the house. He was a missionary and often abroad and it had fallen into some disrepair by the time Miss Alethea Graham bought it in 1961.

Unity House

This house was the home of Digby Latimer, Church Warden from 1850 until 1864. He died in 1884 at the age of 76. Later the Misses Pether lived there, followed by Mr. and Mrs. Yockney—she was the sister of Lord Nuffield, then William Morris. Then came Miss Goodgame, and in 1935 it was bought by the McDowalls, who rented it to Fred Stone, the Hedges and the Wheeler-Booths before they returned to live in it themselves in the early 70s. They have converted part of the old drawing-room into a garage and built on at the back.

North Lodge

The first resident of whom we hear was Mr. Green who ran a small market-garden. He was followed by Mrs. Wheeler, the mother of Jim Wheeler of Mathers farm. In 1941 Mr. and Mrs. Bert Edney bought the house, and after Bert Edney's death in 1960 Alan Edney and his wife moved in with his mother, who died in 1976.

The Grange

Mrs. Masters remembers the Wylies living there, and there are two stained glass windows in the Lady Chapel of St. Andrew's Church put up by them. William Wylie died in 1887, and his widow Ann in 1894. She left the house to her companion Miss Louisa Boss for her life-time. When Miss Boss died at a very advanced age in 1922, the old Wylies' nephew, Robert, moved into the house. He is remembered as walking about the village in an old Norfolk jacket and plus fours. Robert Wylie became one of the first directors of Headington Sports Ground Ltd who bought the fields where the bowling green and football grounds are now. Mrs. Masters says that the Grange was beautifully kept, with scarlet geraniums in the beds outside the house, tended by Bob Cross, the gardener there for many years, who had married the Grange housemaid and lived in 4 St. Andrew's road. Robert Wylie died at the age of 82 in 1948. The Elliot-Smiths bought the house in 1949, and moved in the following year.

There used to be a public footpath to Elsfield through the grounds.

The Priory

The Priory was first called the Lindens (the lime trees on Old High Street belonging to the Manor of Headington). It was originally an Elizabethan house, but Mrs. Masters tells us that General Desborough, when he settled in Old Headington in 1876, rebuilt and spoilt it, adding Victorian windows. The staircase was about all that was left of the old house. The carriage entrance drive was to the south of the house where the new front door has been added. It led round to the original front door facing the garden and then on to the stables to the north. When the Desboroughs left in 1888, the Garth family, with two or three sons lived there. They were followed by the Sturgesses in the early part of the century. Mrs. Sturgess was a widow from Wheatley with 12 children. She lived to be 93. Mrs. Masters remembers with pleasure rehearsing amateur dramatics in the house—the performances taking place in the British Workman.

In the mid-twenties an enclosed order of Dominican Sisters bought the house and since then it has been known as The Priory. The sisters converted the dining-room into their private chapel, and there was a small public chapel near the present side-door, where Mr. Fred Edwards of Larkins Lane acted as server. Near it was a wooden turntable which could be swivelled round so that parcels, bread, etc. could be passed into the convent without personal contact between the sisters and the outside world. Later a Miss Smith, an extern sister who lived in a cottage in the grounds, bought the allotments. Bill Berry was one of the few laymen ever allowed in, once to show the sister in charge of the garden how to work a motor-mower they had been given, and once to kill two of their hens.

Old High Street as it used to be. The Priory was then called the Lindens.

In 1968, The Priory was bought by the Congregation of the Sacred Heart, who came from Barnes in S. W. London. Their main work is teaching, nursing, especially with the mentally handicapped, and doing parish work. Local meetings of Amnesty International and the Catholic Handicapped Children's Fellowship are held in the Priory, as well as many parish meetings. The new front door with two small reception rooms and cloakrooms were added in 1968 and various other alterations made to fit their differing needs from those of the white-robed Dominicans.

The Hermitage

For a long time the Norbury Thomas Knowles family lived here. They were part of the present Oxford firm of builders which was established in 1797. Mrs. Edney told us that they were a great asset to Headington. The three boys all bucked up the sport, playing football etc. They lived there until the young ones were married and after the old people died Mr. Charles F. Bell, Keeper of the Fine Arts at the Ashmolean, bought it in 1912. Of him, Jack Stow recalled that he disliked his windows overlooking the backs of three old stone cottages by his house, so he had them pulled down, about 1920, apparently without warning (see p. 33). There are still marks on the Hermitage wall where the old cottages stood. After the war the Hermitage was empty for some time and then Professor and Mrs. Liddell rented it from Mr. Bell and in the mid-twenties bought it, and have lived there ever since. No alterations to the house have been made.

Bury Knowle

This mansion was built in the early nineteenth century by Sir Joseph Lock, goldsmith and banker, to replace an earlier house. The next owner was George Baker Ballachey who died in 1858. Mrs. Ballachey continued to live there until her death in 1884. It was she who in 1880 gave the ground-site for the present British Workman, and she was very generous in her support of the infant school in North Place. Then came E.B. Fielden, Master of the Foxhounds, and family. He added the brick rear wing to the house, which was then known as The Beeches. At the turn of the century Colonel Kingscote was living in the house. His wife wrote novels under the name of Lucas Cleeve. She was a very charming woman and, as reports have it, very extravagant. Eventually they went bankrupt, having borrowed money from many local people, including George Morris, Vicar of Cowley. Major C.M. Laing and his family then moved in, followed by the Coates and finally the Beaufoys, the pickle people, who were living there during the twenties.

The City Council bought the estate in 1930, and took over the baby health clinic which had been run by volunteers in the British Workman since 1915. This clinic, with doctor and nurse as well as volunteer helpers, has been run twice a week ever since. It was there that orange juice and cod liver oil for young children was collected during and after the Second World War. The public park itself was opened in 1932, and the Branch library in 1934. In 1968 a doctor's surgery was opened, taking the place of one in Sandfield Road.

PUBLIC HOUSES

Public Houses abounded in Old Headington in days gone by. Memories vary, but let us consider the Pub Song, quoted by Jack Stow.

A Black Boy rode a White Horse and carried the Royal Standard shouting 'rule Britannia'. He was chasing a White Hart which had a Bell around its neck. This disturbed the Fox which ran aground in the Prince's Castle.

Some of these inns are now outside Old Headington proper, the White Horse, the Britannia and the Royal Standard being on the London Road, and the Fox, the third of its name, and the Prince's Castle being in Barton. Even this list does not include the Swan, at 8 The Croft, about which Mrs. Masters recalls: 'I can remember the girl there, Edie Taylor. It was a very old public house, with dark panelling and high-backed settles. It was just a beer house, no spirits, and the old men of the village used to go there and smoke their clay pipes.' Charles Taylor, 'a stout man known as Puggler', said Mrs. Coggins, was the publican. Soon after he died in the early twenties, the licence was transferred and it became a private house. Earlier still there was a pub at the present 12 St. Andrew's Road, then Church Street. It was closed through the efforts of Mrs. Ballachey who then lived at Bury Knowle (see p. 30) and was a power in the village in the late nineteenth century. We are also told that the Court was at one time a pub called the Crown and Thistle, much frequented by Oxford undergraduates. Jack Stow said that ' in 1898 a man could enter a pub and buy a pint of beer, 2d., half an ounce Bell tobacco, $1\frac{1}{2}$d. and a box of matches for $\frac{1}{2}$d.'.

The Black Boy was originally a stone cottage at the corner of Old High Street and Barton Lane, in line with a row of old cottages running between it and the present Priory. (The existing mock tudor houses were built by Charlie Morris in 1909.) There was a big elm tree in front of the pub around which the village lads would gather. Jack Stow remembered that near it 'the relief of Mafeking was celebrated by lighting a large bonfire'. Mr. Dennis who was born in 1889 tells us that the first publican he knew was Mr. Carter, who was also a butcher in the Market. Bill Berry speaks of the Bonds as publicans—'I lit my first cigarette with Edward Bond by the hollow oak tree behind the old Black Boy . . .' Mrs. Masters said that in the field behind the pub, which now belongs to the Priory, 'they used to have a feast on Whit Monday'.

After the Bonds, the Grimsleys took over the Black Boy, and a year or so after the end of the First World War Mr. and Mrs. Dickinson moved in. He and his wife Edie (see p. 62) were there throughout the twenties, during which time the City took Old Headington over from Bullingdon and street lamps were installed for the first time. The old Black Boy was pulled down to give more road-room, the new pub being built before the old one came down in the mid-thirties. Mr. Badcock, who had followed the Dickinsons in the old pub, moved over to the new one and stayed there until just before the Second World War. Then came Archie Bolt, and when he died his wife continued as licensee until 1963. Mr. Reg Newman ran the pub until 1975, when Mr. Jackson took it over.

Left: The White Hart garden entrance. *Right:* Jack Williams in the courtyard of the old Bell, showing the path through to the Croft.

The White Hart, perhaps the original 'Joan of Hedington's' alehouse, seems to have changed little over the years. Mrs. Masters described how 'they used to hang up mistletoe at Christmas and take it down next Christmas'. There were mounting stones outside the pub—one still remains in the Croft, near the back entrance. The buildings at that end consisted of stabling for six horses. One can still see the mangers with the open space in the loft above where hay was thrown down to them. Mrs. Coggins remembers that 'the hounds always met outside the church in years gone by. It was quite a picture with the church on one side and the old pub on the other. Beautiful it was. The South Oxford (Hunt) went all round Elsfield and down by the old cottages, which is Dunstan Road now . . . In the old copse down there where Northway is there was a beautiful running stream.'

Charlie Thomas was for a long time the licensee, followed by his son Bill and daughter Jane. Charlie used to keep bantams and bred them for cockfighting. Rumour has it that one bantam cock was especially tame and would sit on customers' arms as they drank their beer. The cock was very attached to its hens, and when its owner moved down to St. Clements it was seen to cling fiercely with its claws to the back of a cat which was approaching its harem too closely. On St. Andrew's Day, we are told by Mr. Dennis, the White Hart used to arrange a big sit-down dinner for the parish.

Mr. Charles Huckin became licensee in about 1950 and stayed until 1963. He was followed by Mr. Hanks who was there for four years before he emigrated to Australia. He took down the partition to the left of the main entrance, which had previously enclosed the 'regulars'' room, where each had his seat. The present licensee, Mr. Maurice Jacobs, comes from Quarry. In 1976 the oak door to the saloon bar from the street was added, and new toilets were built behind. While the foundations were being dug a well was discovered in the back courtyard. It was 26 feet deep and even in 1976—the year of the drought—it contained nine feet of water. Mr. Jacobs wanted to preserve it as a showpiece, but the brewers refused: it is unlikely that it will ever again see the light of day.

The Bell was originally a small beer house facing south, its entrance on a small path joining Old High Street with the Croft. Jack Williams was the landlord, and it was there that Jack Stow, his stepson, was born in 1888. Jack remembered that 'old Mr. Wells, the cab and fly driver, retired . . . lived in an old stone cottage next to the Hermitage. Mr. Wells was frying his breakfast when the cottage was pulled down over his head. My stepfather took Mr. Wells into our pub at the Bell and he lived with us for some time. . . . It was because it was an eyesore to Mr. Bell who lived in the Hermitage.' (See p. 30) This happened soon after the First World War. In the late twenties the Bell was rebuilt and enlarged, but the old pub is still used as the living quarters of the licensees.

For many years the Bell was the headquarters of the Shotover Flying Club until it closed in 1974. Pigeon fanciers met there, and on racing occasions brought their pigeons in baskets and loaded them onto a lorry to be taken to their destination from where the pigeons would race back to their own lofts. In the sixties a pre-fab club house was put up for them in the Bell garden. The old pub stables, with an entrance from the Croft, were used after the Second World War until the mid-sixties for professional boxing training. This was organised by Mr. Sherlock, and the men boxed at fairs and in boxing booths throughout the country.

In 1935, Wilfred Stopps, brother of Alfred Stopps of Church Hill Farm, followed Jack Williams and remained there until 1953 when Mr. J.D. Davies became the licensee.

THE BRITISH WORKMAN

Apart from the public houses, many of the villagers went to the British Workman (65 Old High Street) for relaxation and refreshment. Its motto was 'A public house without the drink where man may sit, talk, read or think and sober home return.' It was the headquarters of the Temperance Society, started in Mrs. Coggins' cottage in The Croft—where in fact she and four generations have been born—and there it stayed until the new British Workman was built in Old High Street in 1880, on land given by Mrs. Ballachey of Bury Knowle and at the expense of Miss Nichol of Jesmond Cottage. As the parish magazine explains it: The new British Workman was 'established for the promotion of three genuine R's, Reading, Recreation and Refreshment, to which may be added a fourth most important R, viz. Religious Instruction.' General Desborough of the Lindens, now the

Priory, was the first chairman. The Band of Hope, the Juvenile Branch of the Temperance Society, flourished here during these years.

In 1883 a large room at the back was added which could hold 200 people or could be partitioned off into three rooms. This addition was the gift of Miss Watson-Taylor of the Manor House. In 1891 a gymnasium for the young people of the parish was built, at a cost of £100, and a qualified instructor came twice a week from Cowley Barracks. Unfortunately the boys were not enthusiastic, and the gymnasium was closed in 1892. During many winters a soup kitchen was provided for villagers. In 1873 soup was a penny a quart; by 1898 it was twopence. Between January and March 1882 this kitchen was open every Wednesday and Friday, during which 1,260 quarts of soup were served to 746 families at a cost of £10.2.0. Coal and clothing clubs were run from the British Workman, and lectures and discussions were also arranged. It was used as a village hall for all kinds of activities.

In the early days of this century Mrs. Coggins tells us that the British Workman was used for dances and whist drives and social occasions, with a room containing two billiard tables. 'When we were girls they held a girls' club there, practising for dancing and all different games.... The caretaker was supposed to be a teetotaller. Only soft drinks and refreshments were supplied. Anyone was allowed to go, and they charged us girls twopence for an evening's pleasure.'

Mr. Percy Cooper, who was born over 70 years ago by the church in one of the thatched cottages demolished in the late thirties (see p. 25), became caretaker of the British Workman just after the Second World War, succeeding Charlie Creese who had followed Mrs. Batts. As a boy he attended carpentry classes there, run twice a week by Mr. George Stace, Senior (see p. 36). Many cottages, of course, had no indoor sanitation or plumbing. But around 1920 an extension was built on to the British Workman in which three public baths were installed, heated by a coal-fired boiler. Mr. Cooper remembers having his weekly bath there as a boy, while others remember their being used during the Second World War. The baths were dismantled in 1946 when the room so used was converted by Mr. Cooper into his kitchen.

In 1915 a voluntary committee was set up to provide facilities for mothers to bring their babies for weighing, professional advice, etc. This baby health clinic continued in the British Workman until 1930 when it was transferred to Bury Knowle and the City took it over. During the Second World War and after, ration books were distributed from the British Workman, and it was also the Home Guard's headquarters.

Throughout this century it was the centre of most of the village sporting activities. Committee meetings and social evenings were held there right up to and beyond the time in the fifties when Headington Football Club became professional, first as Headington United and then as Oxford United. It was also the Cricket Club centre, Mr. Bradley of Barton End having given the village the cricket ground in Barton Road. Billiards, darts, table tennis were all played there.

In the sixties, the old malthouse—which is the flat-roofed building to the south—and the old gymnasium behind it, were leased to Viking Sports and have become the headquarters of its table-tennis section. About 40 to 50 junior members are coached there by

Mr. Harvey Harries who is an E.T.T.A. club coach and is also their chairman. Of the 42 players in the 14 teams of the local League, 30 are aged 18 and under and are coached at the British Workman. At present 75 per cent of their members come from the Headington area.

It was in the sixties that Bingo sessions were started here. They are held three times a week.

SCHOOLS

The schools are often mentioned in the parish magazines. The first master of the National School in Headington had been Mr. John Bird, and he had held the post for 12 years. Then due to ill health he had gone to South Africa where he died in 1870, aged 63.

In 1869 Mr. Vallis was headmaster and Mrs. Vallis schoolmistress of the National School. Each scholar paid 2d weekly. At this time there were 64 boys and 62 girls on the books. There was also a Sunday School and a night school, which met at 7 p.m. in the evening on Mondays and Wednesdays. Finally there was an infants school, where there were 60 pupils, and one penny was paid weekly for the first child and a half penny for every other child from the same family.

Each August the children of the National School had their annual treat. On 11 August 1869 they assembled in the school for prayer, and then marched in procession to Mrs. Ballachey's grounds in Bury Knowle. Tea was served by Mr. Wyatt (licensee of the White Hart) and 70 girls and 62 boys were present. After tea all the parents joined in and they played cricket and other games. At 8 o'clock prizes were given to those who had attended school 'very frequently'.

The income for the school came in by annual subscription, part paid by the parish, part by the scholars, and the government grant contributed £42. In 1870, on the expenditure side, the teachers received £96. £1.6.1. was paid for books and stationery, £4.14.0 on fuel and other small items. Mr. Vallis had been the headmaster for only two years when he died unexpectedly.

In 1871 the report of the H.M. Inspector of Headington National Schools complained much of the very irregular attendance of the children at the day school. Out of 120 boys and girls, only 70 were qualified by their attendance for examination. Of the 51 who were actually presented, 24 passed in reading, 16 in writing, and 23 in arithmetic. The government grant for the day school was £43.16s, of which sum £31.4s was allowed for attendance, and £12.12s for examination. The grant for the night school was £8.6.8, viz £3.15s for attendance and £4.11.8 for examination. 26 scholars were presented for examination, of whom 17 passed in reading, 20 in writing and 18 in arithmetic.

In 1875 the boys' head teacher was Mr. Thomas Yeates, and the girls' headmistress was Miss Harriet Crozier. Children in the Infants School in North Place, Old Headington, were taught by Miss Mary Ann Crozier, and Mrs. Vallis was at the Infants' School, New Headington, which had been built in 1874 for £441.

In 1887 the school fees for labourers whose weekly earnings were under £1 were 3d a week for the first child and 2d for others. Those who earned over £1 had to pay 4d for the first child and 3d for others. Those who were assessed to the poor-rate at or over £10 had to pay 6d a week for every child.

In 1891 free education came into force. This meant that the children no longer had to pay for attendance at school. Instead the Government gave grants to cover the amount. A voluntary rate from the village was still provided to maintain them as Church schools. The change-over was not finalised until 1893.

In 1893 and 1894 the parish had to collect money to build new schools in the London Road. The estimate for the building itself was £1,912, but extras including architects' fees, boundary wall and furniture etc. meant that about £300 more would be needed. The Bishop of Oxford laid the foundation stone on 12 June 1894 (when the buildings were already well in hand), and by then £1,700 had been raised. It was hoped that everything would be completed by the beginning of the school year, and that the old school building behind could then be adapted for the infants' use. On St. Andrew's Day the schools were officially opened, and supper for 230 was served in the new schools. Henceforward many dances and concerts, etc. were held there rather than in the British Workman (see p. 33). So much for the records.

Everyone we have talked to remembers the kindergarten school in the tin hut adjoining 41 St. Andrew's Road, opposite the Parish Hall, which many of the older inhabitants attended. Mrs. Masters refers to it as 'an old dame school', and when Bill Berry went to it at the age of 6, it had 25 children. Jack Stow went there at the age of 3 in 1891. Miss Steff was the only teacher, and she taught music and used to charge 6d an hour. It was not shut down until the late nineteen twenties. On leaving Miss Steff's school most of the children went on to the Infants School in North Place where since 1873 the Headmistress had been Mrs. Crozier. Before 1873 the Infants School was known as Mrs. Ballachey's school and was 'for many years entirely supported by that lady'. Then the Government took it over, although Mrs. Ballachey continued to contribute £20 a year. Parents were urged to send their children there, otherwise there would have to be 'a compulsory system of education', in which a School Board would be in charge and no religious training given.

But who better can there be to tell us more about the National Schools of Headington than George Stace? He had been Headmaster of St. Andrew's School (or the Field School) from 1921 to 1952 as his father was from 1879 to 1921. This is what the son told us a few years ago–

'My father was born in Woolwich, and on coming to Headington Village will be remembered by some as the organist and choirmaster of St. Andrew's Church under Mr. Tyndale and Mr. Scott Tucker, the Vicars during the period. He was a strict disciplinarian, and he had a good choir of some ten to twelve boys, with ten men. Apart from being a good Headmaster, he was also an excellent cabinet maker and I have at Church Hanborough a collection of the furniture that he made which is extremely decorative and beautiful. He was a keen cyclist, as were other members of the family, and he won a medal for riding an old penny-farthing bike on the London to Brighton race. On this it was inscribed that he was champion of the Imperial Bicycle Club for 1878. In 1921, when he retired, he was given with his present, a list of contributors, with their names all beautifully inscribed in copper plate.' In that list there are such names as Mr. and Mrs. W.J. Berry, Mr. and Mrs. H.E. Berry, Mr. and Mrs. J.W. Berry, Mr. Percy Copper, the Misses Davenport, quite a few Hedges, half a page of Jacobs, Mr. Frank Jeffs, Mrs. G. Louch, Mrs. W. Louch, six or seven Mattocks, Mr. Jack Stow, Mr. Gilbert Taylor, Mr. Arthur Vallis, Mr. and Mrs. A. Webb, Miss Wootten-Wootten, Miss A. Wootten-Wootten, and so on. Many of those names will be very familiar.

George Stace, Jr. was born in 1887, in Lime Walk, one of a family of four children, two boys and two girls. When he was a baby the family moved to Windmill Road. George went to the infants school in North Place, under Mrs. Crozier. Margaret Stace went to New Headington Infants School, held in the parish room of All Saints Church nearby. George then went on to his father's school, the Headington National School or St. Andrew's School, where there were 150 boys, with separate departments for the boys and the girls. London Road in those days was just a country road, with no houses between the Co-op and the school, and nothing between the school and the Laurels, the old workhouse near what is now Shotover roundabout. When he was ten he used to play cricket and football in the middle of the main London road. This was allowed by the Headmaster, as there was so little traffic. The odd carrier's cart came along from Beckley, and George remembered that on one very special occasion Barnum and Bailey's circus came through Oxford. His father asked one of the boys to go and buy two loaves so that the school boys could feed the elephants as they passed.

The Rocket. Headington to Oxford, 6d. return.

There were no scholarships in those days; George's brother went to Oxford University, and George, who felt he was much better at using his hands than his head, was told by his father that as he had to do something, he had better be a teacher. He went on to the pupil teachers' centre in New Inn Hall Street, which he attended twice a week, and he often did school practice in St. Andrew's School in the mornings. He sat for the King's Scholarship Examination at 18, and went on to Culham College in 1908 for two years. Then he was assistant master at Bicester for two years. After that he came back to Headington, to Margaret Road School, until 1914. He spent a short period as Headmaster of Quarry School just before joining the Royal Flying Corps. On his demobilisation in 1919 he became Headmaster at Fringford, near Bicester. Two years later his father retired and George took over from him as Headmaster of St. Andrew's School, where he remained until 1952.

Miss Margaret Stace went on from St. Andrew's School to Milham Ford School, then in Cowley Place, under Miss Dodds, the Headmistress. Later she came back and joined her father and was on the regular staff of St. Andrew's School. The family remained in Windmill Road until 1928, when their father died. They then moved to Field House in the London Road, at Sandhills, and later to Shotover. When George Stace retired in 1952, they went to Church Hanborough.

St. Andrew's School had a good record for athletics, and during the Staces' time held many prizes and trophies. George Stace senior had a reputation for discipline, but, as he said, it was necessary, 'as there were funny goings on in those days'. Most boys and girls left at the age of 13, and they took jobs on the land, in the gardens, or as errand boys or domestic servants.

Needlework at St. Andrew's School was usually taught by ladies from the village who came in to help, and one of them was Miss Wootten. At the top of Old High Street, where there are now two houses standing back, and which back onto the new car park, there used to be one cottage, Ivy Cottage, in which George Stace's great aunts lived. They were his mother's aunts, Thirsa and Hannah. It was with them that George Stace, Sr. had lodged, and where Kate Grant, on a visit from her home at Sidmouth, had met him. Later they were married.

The son George was a keen cyclist before he changed to motor bikes. He was a motor bike pioneer and he and Knowles the builder in Old High Street were the only two people in the neighbourhood who had them in 1914. George bought his first motor bike from Dr. Hitchings second-hand for £30 but had to satisfy the doctor that he could drive it round his garden for twenty minutes before he was let loose to drive to Stanton St. John. He had his licence, but in those days there was no insurance or driving test. He then went on to a superior bike for which he paid £100, then had a super sports Morgan and later a bull-nosed Morris, in which he took his mother about for many years. After that he bought a Jaguar for £110. Cars were few and far between, but Miss Price at the Rookery had an old Daimler. George won prizes in all sorts of motor cycle races, including the London to Edinburgh race, the London to Lands End race, and the race from London to Gloucester and back. Later he took to racing with a side car, with his sister as passenger.

Bill Kimber was very well known to the family, and indeed taught them all dancing.

Miss Mabel Stace became a great specialist in country dancing. Mark Cox, who probably originated the Morris Dancers, had a son at the school whom George remembers well. During George Stace's time the managers of the school were the Vicar, Miss Clarke, Mr. Dockray of Stoke, Mr. George Morrell, and Mr. Laing of Bury Knowle.

George remembered the first motor buses, William Morris having one fleet and Tyrells having another. The buses were double deckers, and had great difficulty in getting up Headington Hill. There was another means of transport, in earlier days. Mr. Dring had a two-horse brake, called the Rocket, which went to Oxford once or twice a day. The Rocket needed two extra horses to pull it up the hill, and these were kept at St. Clements. The four horses pulled the Rocket up the hill, and two horses were then taken off to reinforce the next Rocket up. Another way was to walk across the field down Divinity Road to Cowley Road, and catch the horse tram along the Cowley Road to the Plain.

Miss Agnes Janet Levett, who lived at 74, Old High Street, until her death on 4 September 1975 at the age of 101, was born in Pumpkin Cottage in St. Andrew's Lane. Her father was the gardener at North Lodge. She served under Miss Elizabeth Drake, the girls' Headmistress, later to become Mrs. John Mattock, then under Miss Hewitt and then under Mrs. Bridgewater, all at the Field School, now St. Andrew's School.

For years the Field School was known as St. Andrew's C. of E. Primary School but from 1975 it has been known officially as St. Andrew's First School.

Apart from the National Schools there have been several private schools in addition to Miss Steff's. There was Dr. Gibson's preparatory school at the Rookery from 1880 onwards. There was another run by Miss Mabel Edney in her own home at 84 Old High Street in the 1920s, with about fifteen children of 5–7 years paying 1s.6d–2s.6d a week for tuition. We know of one pageant produced by Miss Wellbourne (see p. 14) and performed at Headington House in which some of these children took part.

But there were also those for young children run by Miss Katharine Woods and Miss Margaret Hamersley. This is what they told us–

Miss K. Woods and her family came to Headington in 1915 so that she herself could go to the University. They lived in a little semi-detached house in London Road, whence they could see Wittenham Clumps from the top windows. After the war they decided to buy a plot in Osler Road, in memory of her brother, and Hunsdon House Garden School was built on it. Miss Woods had already started teaching two children in the dining room, and when numbers grew to 15, she rented Mrs. Blackburn's garden room in London Road (now Horwood Close). Then the wooden school was put up. Hunsdon House was built with windows and doors which could open wide to the south and east. Vita glass was used. Educationists from Birmingham came to look at the school to make their own nursery schools on the same model. Miss Woods felt that formal work should be linked with something that was real and interesting to the children, especially during their early impressionable years, and also that the rates of development of the children should be taken into account.

In 1931 the school was inspected by the Board of Education which gave it a very fine report: 'fifteen children in the school aged two to eight, the staff well qualified for the work, and the children happy and high spirited, busy with definite well-planned work.' Under

Left: Some pupils of Miss Edney's school in a pageant at Headington House. *Right:* 1908 Sunday School outing in Old High Street, with the Wootten estate behind.

Mr. and Mrs. Archie Utin, who were there until 1974, the school carried on the policy very happily, though using more painting than music.

In 1974 when the Utins retired Mrs. Rosemarie Deepwell took over Hunsdon House. She now has up to 36 children in all and is carrying on the tradition of this popular nursery school.

Miss M. Hamersley came to Headington in 1927 and went to school in Oxford. In 1930 she worked for a time as a pupil teacher at Hunsdon House. Her father had been a land agent in Leicestershire, but had spent his youth in South Oxfordshire, and he wished to come back to his old county. The family lived at Sandy Lodge for 25 years. Miss Hamersley went as a teacher to Queen Margaret School in Yorkshire for a year or two, then she returned to Sandy Lodge and started teaching three children in a hut in the garden. The class soon grew to twelve, which was as many as she could take. When the Second World War broke out, she joined the Red Cross. But in 1946 Sandy Lodge became a school again, and she ran it until 1959. Among her pupils have been Lord Elton's son Rodney, and Sue McGregor of B.B.C. Woman's Hour. In the winter she produced a nativity play, and in the summer sports and cricket matches, in which the parents joined. Sometimes little plays were performed in the summer too.

Miss Hamersley remembers White Lodge as the place where Headington School was born, about 1916. With Miss Porcher in charge it moved to Napier House, and in the early 1930s the present school was built. She feels that the village has remained very much as it was when she first came in 1927.

Ormerod School for many years was a rather special institution in Old Headington.

In 1901 that eminent physician and great humanitarian, Dr. Arthur Latham Ormerod, was appointed the first full-time medical Officer of Health for Oxford, a post which he filled with distinction until 1929. By dint of constant concern and hard work, he improved the Public Health provisions in Oxford in every area of activity, and as these improved under his direction Dr. Ormerod managed to give extra time to medical inspection and care of school children. At his instigation an open-air school was opened in 1928 in the Manor House grounds acquired by the Radcliffe Infirmary at Headington, the site of the Osler Hospital and now of the John Radcliffe Hospital.

In its early days the 'Open-Air School' catered for 40 children in the winter and 50 in the summer, aged 8–11 years, on a daily non-resident basis. In its first fifteen months 61 children had been admitted and 25 had been returned, much improved, to ordinary schools. Most of the children suffered from tuberculosis and related diseases, but over the years the position changed. By 1955 the role of 'The Open-Air School' was more of a school for children with physical handicaps severe enough for them to be unable to cope with the programme of ordinary schools.

Today Ormerod School, as the Open-Air School was renamed in 1959, caters for physically handicapped children between the ages of 6 and 16 on a daily non-resident basis. It has some 45 children of varying degrees of disability drawn from the City and from the villages of Oxfordshire and North Berkshire. The object is to provide an education to enable them to take part in the life of the community around them and they have a dedicated headmistress and a small devoted staff working to this end.

The children are neither intellectually nor educationally sub-normal in spite of difficulties in communication and self-expression. As they develop, some move to ordinary schools and even to upper schools.

The local authority does all it can to help with the provision of special equipment, but there are other needs which can only be met with the help of the outside community. A small body called the Friends of Ormerod School assists in fund-raising, giving time, friendship, affection and 'outside' interest to the rather limited social life of the children.

In 1976 the school was moved to a new building at Barton with accommodation for some 120 children of all ages plus a nursery unit for 20.

WOMEN'S INSTITUTES

For much of what is given under this heading we are indebted to Miss K. Woods, who has written a booklet on the subject.

Women's Institutes came to England from Canada in 1915. In 1918 Miss Woods and others went visiting all round Headington to discover what response there would be for a Headington Women's Institute. (Old Headington, Highfield and Quarry all had the same

Parish Council.) On 25 April 1918 the Headington Women's Institute was formed, and monthly meetings thereafter were held at the British Workman in Old High Street. After five years Quarry members decided to form their own W.I. in Quarry. Several years later Headington W.I. had to find a new home, and so moved across to Highfield. Then in 1962, Old Headington took advantage of the newly built St. Andrew's Parish Hall, and formed its own Institute with Mrs. Elizabeth Cameron—Elizabeth Bowen, the novelist—as President. Many years earlier she had been President of Headington W.I. and the connection between the two Institutes remained close.

Several of the keenest and most active members of Old Headington W.I. are daughters and nieces of these early pioneers, who included Mrs. Harry Berry, Mrs. Stopps, and Mrs. William Mattock, whose daughter Mrs. Iris Masters joined in 1919. Mrs. Masters is a real countrywoman—she remembers her grandfather in his shepherd's smock when he owned a flock of sheep in Elsfield. She used to watch her grandmother sitting smocking at her open door, and featherstitching the shepherd's crook, the mark of his trade, in white on the unbleached linen smock. She is widely known for her contributions to Institute skills, and in 1920 she won the Gold Medal for preserved fruit at the Oxfordshire Agricultural Show. Four years later she gained an open exhibition for a residential course in canning and bottling at the Campden Canning Station. Her diploma qualified her to demonstrate and to teach for the County, and many W.I.s have benefited by her knowledge and skill.

Drama and music have always been important in the Headington W.I.s. The first play

W.I. War Kitchen, London Road, 1918.

was produced by Miss Shelford of Monkton Cottage, Old High Street. She lent her kitchen for rehearsals and the play was performed in the British Workman. It was a great success. In 1925 and again in the early thirties when she was President, Mrs. Cameron gave great encouragement to W.I. Drama, producing plays for the Oxford Federation of Women's Institutes. One of the funniest was *The Morning of the Wedding*, performed at a Dramatic Festival at Islip.

Mrs. Oliver West, now Mrs. Pearce, kept up the interest with original and colourful productions. And in the sixties the Old Headington W.I., encouraged by Mrs. Cameron who was then living at White Lodge, produced some delightful out-door pageantry in which any Old Headington children who cared to do so were invited to take part.

Miss Margaret and Miss Helena Deneke were members of the Headington W.I. and pioneered musical appreciation in the Institutes of Oxfordshire. Mrs. Gwen Archer kept up the musical interests of the W.I.s and has helped to organise some excellent musical evenings.

In handicrafts the Institutes have been active. The first Headington W.I. President, Mrs. Olive Jacks, took a keen interest in weaving and other crafts. She introduced a pillow-lace maker to teach in the Institutes, and helped a skilled weaver to come from Kent and set up in Kiln Lane. Miss May Morris, daughter of William Morris, came to talk to the Institute about his work in the art of tapestry weaving, wall-paper printing and book design in the early twenties.

FARMS AND FARMING

One must realise that Old Headington, anyway until the First World War and largely until the end of the twenties when the Northern By-pass was built, was a village surrounded by farmland and worked by tenant farmers.

Mathers Farm, owned by Magdalen College, in the 1880s was farmed by William Berry, who came from Islip. His fields lay where the present Chestnut/Hawthorn Avenue now stand and ran right across towards Wick Farm. On William Berry's death in 1888 his widow, Sarah Ann Berry, and young family stayed on in the house and the baking business was carried on there. The fields, however, were farmed first by Joe Stringer of Barton Farm, and later by Jim Wheeler, famous for his dairy shorthorns, who moved into Mathers Farm when the Berry family went to the present bakery early in the First World War. He stayed there until after the Second World War. Most of the land was pasture, but there was one arable field on the right of Barton Lane. The big barn—now converted to a house—was used for threshing.

After the Second World War, the house was occupied by various members of Magdalen College. It was sold in the late sixties.

Church Hill Farm, where William Orchard Close now stands, was owned by Mr. Wylie of the Grange. Early this century it was a dairy farm run first by Mr. Wheeler, followed by Bill Cooke and then by the Stopps family who retailed milk. When the by-pass was built and the cows could no longer easily cross it the farm gradually deteriorated. The farmhouse itself (4 St. Andrew's Lane) was sold by the Church Hill Farm Trustees (see p. 48) to Mr. F. Ricketts who has restored it beautifully.

Laurel Farm was where the Woottens' cowman lived. Until the break-up of the estate, he was in charge of the jersey cows in the meadows to the south of Headington House. The milk was put in large pans and the cream and butter made from it were for the personal use of the Wootten family. During and after the First World War, when it belonged to Corpus Christi College, it was leased by Mrs. Jones, later to become Mrs. Tagg, who ran it as a flourishing nursery garden.

Highfield. Mr. Hathaway senior came from London in 1903 and began milk retailing in a small way from Lime Walk. The cows were kept there throughout the winter. Soon he extended his business and rented the Wootten meadows between Old High Street and Osler Road before the houses were built in the twenties. They had about 20 cows there. There were eight cowsheds on the south side of Headington House drive, which were reached by the bridge over Cuckoo Lane, and a small threshing machine. At one time the Hathaways grew corn on the fields to the east of St. Andrew's School and root crops where the present Headington Girls' School stands for winter feeding their cattle and horses. Later, when these fields were sold for building, they rented some fields in Northway where the little park is now.

After the First World War when Harry Hathaway, who supplied this information, came out of the Navy, his father gave him a milk float made by Mr. Corby of Quarry. It cost £50. There were in all three milk-floats with horses, and twice a day they delivered milk warm from the cow (there being no pasteurisation) all round Headington and Quarry. It cost $\frac{1}{2}$d a quarter pint during the twenties and thirties, and on Sundays skimmed milk was sold at 2d. a quart. During the Second World War the Co-op started delivering milk. The Hathaways gave up the farm but for a time continued retailing milk supplied by Jim Wheeler at Mathers. Soon after the war they sold up to Burtons Dairy.

Lower Farm in 1906, when Harry Berry took it over from Mr. Soloway, was first rented from the Wootten family and then from Mr. Stowe of West Lodge (see p. 24) who bought the farm in 1912. In 1926, on Mr. Stowe's death, Harry Berry bought the farm and grounds—roughly 65 acres. Harry Berry was a trained butcher with a shop in Old High Street. (See p. 46) He killed his own cattle for sale. His fields stretched across the present by-pass towards Elsfield.

Manor Farm, where the John Radcliffe Hospital now stands, was farmed by Mr. and Mrs. Hartwell for William Peppercorn, Lord of the Manor, and at the turn of the century by John Wiggins. There was a fire at the farm in 1897 and the fire engines drawn by horses were brought up from Oxford. As a child, Mrs. Coggins, whose father worked there, used to fetch the milk from Mr. Wiggins for the family, there being no milk delivery. In the twenties Tom White, whose father William farmed Wood Farm off the Slade, used the grounds for extra pasture. He sold his milk wholesale rather than retailing it. Tom White first lived in Cemetery Cottage, but moved to Barton Farm, opposite the Prince's Castle in the twenties and the Brown family—whose son Dick worked at the Rookery—lived in the cottage. Mr. Brown senior was 'carter' in Tom White's employ.

The Manor Farm House early this century.

SHOPS

The Post Office, at the corner of Old High Street and St. Andrew's Road (then Church St.) used to be the centre of the village in many ways. The Rudds were already there in 1879. The first telegrams were sent out by horse and cart and there is still a ring in the back yard to which the horse to deliver them could be attached. For many years it contained the only public telephone of the village—and there were very few private ones. Groceries were also sold, and all the oddments of a village shop.

Before the First World War Harold Rudd moved up to London Road where a Post Office was opened at the western corner of Windmill Road and London Road. Then the Gillivers took over the Old Headington shop. Mr. Bill Berry remembers helping the daughters to make ice cream in the summer—a long and laborious job in those days. The Gillivers were followed by Bill Wheeler, who had been a gardener at Headington House. He sold stamps as well as groceries. He remained there until his death after the Second World War. After Mr. Braben's short occupancy Mrs. Bond ran the shop until 1965 when she retired and the shop, as such, was closed.

Berry the Baker's first shop was in Mathers Farm. It was run by Mrs. Sarah Berry until her son William Berry was old enough to take it over. Early in the First World War the family had to vacate Mathers and moved over to the present site, building the present bakery in the garden. There they have remained ever since.

86 Old High Street was at one time a fish shop, run by Mr. Warren, who had been a coachman to Colonel Hoole. He also sold sausages. This was later taken over by Mr. Oram.

H.E. Berry's Butcher's shop at 82 Old High Street was opened in 1908, meat being sold on the left and sweets on the right of the shop. Allen's, who had a grocery shop in the London Road, took it over in the sixties, and now it is a store room for Berry the Baker's.

76 Old High Street was run by Mr. Williams, a pork butcher. Later Mrs. Somerville, Miss Levett's mother, took it over and sold sweets and vegetables grown by her husband on the ground where the present car park stands behind Bury Knowle.

We are also told of two other sweet shops, Mrs. Tempero's in 2 St. Andrew's Lane, with the bay window, and Sally North's in North Place.

Headington Produce, where the new house has been built at 55 Old High Street, was a greengrocer after the Second World War and then turned to general grocery until 1972.

EXPANSION AND CONSERVATION

It was during the twenties, after the Wootten-Wootten estate and the Manor House ground were sold up, that the semi-detached houses of Old High Street and Osler Road were built. London Road became more of a shopping centre on its north side. Stephen Road and the housing estate between Barton Lane and London Road emerged. Old Headington was on the verge of becoming a suburb of Oxford, the City finally taking it over in 1929.

In the village proper a few new houses also appeared. In the late twenties Lord Elton, a University don, built Greenways (40 Osler Road). His young son went to Miss Hamersley's school at Sandy Lodge. The Eltons left to go to Adderbury in the late forties. After a short occupancy by a director of Pressed Steel, Mr. Mulgan, a New Zealander, bought the house. He was a property developer but his overriding interest was music. He and his family lived there until 1960, when Dr. R.G. Anderson sold old Dr. Hitchings' house, Headington Cottage, in London Road to Fine Fare, and bought Greenways. In the early seventies the Andersons moved again to 38 Osler Road, the old lodge of the Wootten estate, having first enlarged and modernised it. John Johnson, Printer to the University, built Bareacres in Barton Lane, also in the twenties. This was bought by the ter Haars in the sixties when John Johnson's widow left Old Headington. In the thirties four houses on the south side of Dunstan Road were put up, the first being Dunstan Cottage which was built for Dr. Emden's mother, and where he himself now lives. It was at this time that the old name of Cemetery Lane was changed to Dunstan Road.

After the Second World War, the first house to be built was 4 Dunstan Road, on part of the Rookery ground retained by Mr. Gurden when he sold the Rookery to Ruskin College (p. 24). This was built for his daughter Audrey and her husband John Willis in the late forties. Then it became the turn of Stoke Place. In the mid-fifties Mr. and Mrs. Little built their bungalow 'Denstoke', owned later by the Mintys and now by the Grays and renamed 'Baraka'. Major-General Melville-Lee of Stoke sold the Littles the land which was in the

Green Belt. His son, Colonel Melville-Lee, sold sites for three more houses in Stoke Place and Ruskin built Rookery Cottage in their own grounds.

By the early 1950s the Northway Estate was developing so Dunstan Road no longer petered out at the cemetery: the old footpaths became a road to Copse Lane.

In the fifties the need for a parish hall became urgent, and the field at the corner of St. Andrew's Road and Dunstan Road was bought for St. Andrew's Church from the Hospital authorities. Weekly collections round the parish were made for some years and many money-raising schemes were put in hand. In 1958 the new St. Andrew's Hall was opened. The City Council agreed to build a stone wall in exchange for the land between it and the road so that the corner would be safer for traffic.

So far additions to the village had not been extensive, but in 1959 a serious threat to the village emerged. A company of outside developers bought from Mr. Wylie's executors (see The Grange, p. 28) the field north of the church. It was felt very strongly that an unsympathetic estate on that site, extending possibly into the Green Belt, would be a disaster. Various residents got together, invited the whole village to a meeting in the Parish Hall, and the Friends of Old Headington came into being. A committee was elected, Dr. A.B. Emden agreed to be President and the original Vice-Presidents were Sir Isaiah Berlin, Alderman Frank Pickstock and Mr. S.J. Kingerlee.

For many years the Friends coped untiringly with various unsuitable plans submitted by Span Developments. In 1963 there was an appeal in the Town Hall in which the City Council and the Friends of Old Headington, represented by a Q.C., opposed the latest Span

21 St. Andrew's Lane before and after restoration.

plan. The result was a technical victory for the Council and Old Headington. Then in 1965 the developers, perhaps fed up with the fight, offered to sell the land to the Friends for £14,000. The village took up the challenge. Individual residents were approached to lend money at a low rate of interest. So the Church Hill Farm Trustees came into being and bought the field. The result was that in 1967 the building of the new William Orchard Close was started, and its plan ensured that no additions could be made to the five houses.

Other new houses built were 7 The Croft in 1963; two houses on the south side of Dunstan Road next to the cemetery in 1967; five houses and one bungalow in Ethelred Court between 1967 and 1969; the 'fortress' development of five houses on the north of Dunstan Road in 1968; 39A St. Andrew's Road in 1970; 62 Osler Road in 1970–72; and 'Ebor' in Dunstan Road in 1973.

Some interesting restorations and conversions have also been made in the village. In 1969–70, Mr. and Mrs. D.S. Frith largely rebuilt 21 St. Andrew's Lane, which was in ruins. A little later the Manor Farm House stables were converted into a bungalow for Mr. and Mrs. E.C. Oak. In 1974–5 the barn in Barton Lane, once belonging to Mathers Farm and having passed through various hands, was bought by Mr. Ian Heggie. He has converted it into a most exciting residence for his family. And the house at the south corner of Old High Street and North Place has been partly rebuilt and partly converted into

Inside the restored Barn in Barton Lane.

two dwellings, 55A Old High Street and 1A North Place. The Oxford Preservation Trust on their fiftieth Anniversary in 1977 gave awards to three of these and a certificate to Mr. Oak. The old stable buildings to the east of Larkins Lane were largely rebuilt and converted in 1976–77, and the house is now named Meadow Larkin. Finally the old schoolhouse, 3 North Place, has been successfully restored and enlarged.

In 1971 Old Headington became officially recognised by the City Council as a Conservation Area, and all suggested additions are carefully scrutinised. This should mean that its village atmosphere, with its lanes, walls, trees and grass verges can be preserved and that new buildings and alterations will be in keeping with its existing character. The Friends of Old Headington endeavour to keep an ever-watchful eye on the village, and they look for continuing co-operation and support from the whole community if Old Headington is to keep its village character.

A garden in the Croft.

PART 2: *Village Memories*

VILLAGE MEMORIES

Mr. Bert Edney

We get a good idea of the village in days gone by from a letter written in 1953 by Mr. Bert Edney—husband of Alice Edney née Berry (see below)—of North Lodge, Church Lane, when he was about 74 years old. He writes 'I remember when the village of Old Headington was small, and surrounded by farms and countryside. Old High Street, Church Street, the Croft, Church Lane and Larkins Lane completed the village, with the exception of a few outlying cottages. The Rev. Scott Tucker was the vicar (1889–99). He was a great sportsman and a prominent figure. The Manor House was owned by Colonel Hoole, Bury Knowle by Mrs. Kingscote, and Headington House by Woottens, the bankers.

'The roads and foot-paths were mostly unmade, no sewerage, no street lighting, and the only transport to Oxford was a hansom cab owned by Mr. Webb, who lived in Old High Street, and who was the milkman. The centre of recreation was the British Workman Club in Old High Street, of which the motto is "where man may sit, talk, read or think and sober home return". There was a club with a gymnasium for men and youths, where cards and indoor games would be played. Saturday night was a special sing-song night, and a large company could be found round a fire with supper supplied by the caretaker, no intoxicating drink being allowed.

'Headington always possessed good sportsmen, and the cricket and football teams were tough competitors. The ground was at the end of Manor Road, now Osler Road, but then called Sandy Lane, in Colonel Hoole's paddock. On August Bank Holiday sports for all were held in Woottens' Park, the ground bordered by Old High Street, London Road and Manor Road. This was a beautiful park, surrounded by trees, and the occasion was always a day out for Headington. A minstrel troupe was formed in the village, and many concerts were given, which proved very popular. At Christmas time the village waits were a festive sight; the names of Tolley, Callaway and Burke will be remembered by some. The infants' school was in North Place, on the left of the entrance to Bury Knowle Park, where the school house still stands.'

Mrs. Edney, Senior

Mrs. Edney, the sister of William Berry who ran the bakery business and of Harry Berry, who opened a butcher's shop in Old High Street, and Auntie Al. as she was affectionately known by the Berry family, lived at North Lodge, St. Andrew's Lane, and she had a very long memory. Her first comment was 'I remember very well Mafeking night when the old tree in front of the Black Boy was burnt as a result of the jollifications'. Then she went on 'all the roads were muddy, no macadam in those days, no electric light, no gas, all dark streets, and we had oil lamps. We were a big family, and when we started school, after we had finished with the infants' school, we went to the Field School. We would go by the turnpike at the top of Old High Street, and on the other side was Wootten Park' (see Headington House, p. 20).

'When my father died (in 1888), the boys of course were not old enough to manage the farm, Mathers, so the stock had to be sold, but we were allowed to live on in the house. Mr. and Mrs. Wheeler were then farming in Church Hill Farm. Their land joined Mathers. so they farmed the land, but we children were allowed the run of the meadows. Much later, my mother left Headington, and my brother Will, Bill and Ken's father, managed the business.

'When I married Bert Edney and left Mathers Farm in 1908, my husband and I bought our little house, built by Charlie Morris in Windmill Road, called Headlands, right at the top opposite the present Nuffield. Alan was born a year after and Roger three years after that. We started our business [Edney and Son, Tailors] in London Road, after the first war in 1920 and lived over the shop. We worked very hard. I lived in Headington all my life, I have never been away for any length of time. We moved back here [North Lodge] in 1941.

'When my father died Mr. Tyndale was vicar, and he had three daughters, with lovely names, Mary, Marcia and Auriol, and a son Henry. The Rev. Scott Tucker came when Mr.

Mathers Farm when it was the bakery.

Tyndale went. When we were at Sunday School, we used to see all the different families coming to church. The Davenports would come, the Napiers, Sir William Markby with his wife, and so on. Miss Clarke, who lived at 10 St. Andrew's Road was a musical lady and played the harmonium down at the Mission Church. I remember all about the north aisle, and the cost which was about £700 which they collected in two years. When it went up we could not sit in our usual places for the morning service, so instead of that we used to go to the little Mission Church which was used for services for children. It is now the scout hall in Highfield.

'Quite a lot of the old cottages have disappeared entirely. There was a cobbled sort of yard towards Headington House, and there were two cottages, where Cox the coachman lived, and the Wingfields. Mr. Wingfield was the dairyman. The present Lodge used not to be there.

'Mr. Tyndale, and his three daughters were very kind to my mother and to all of us. Mr. Tuckwell, the curate, was a marvellous man and very much loved. He went blind, you know, and was a great musician. He remained a bachelor.

'I remember Mrs. Coggins and her sister who went to school with me, and Mrs. Flack, and of course Miss Levett, (see Schools). She taught me when she was a pupil teacher for a time. Miss Elizabeth Drake was the headmistress at the Field School and she became Mrs. John Mattock. Then Miss Hewitt came, and after her Mrs. Bridgewater. I remember Gertie Hedges' parents, when they lived in the cottage opposite the church [16, St. Andrew's Road]. My father met my mother for the first time at a wedding which took place in the big meadow cottage where old Mrs. Godfrey lived: it is down now, and my mother was married from there. Old Sam Smith lived on the Bank—it was called the Bank—there is a bank as you know, and he was Sylvia Parker's grandfather. Dr. Massie built that house for his gardener, Mr. Dawes, but it was much smaller, only a little cottage [39 St. Andrew's Road]. We used to go down to Manor Farm for milk when our farm had to go. Mr. and Mrs. Hartwell were there, and kept cattle. They were related to the Wiggins family.

'Sam West, the florist, had the Close before the Douglases, at the turn of the century. Another brother West lived higher up Old High Street. He owned all Westbourne Terrace, and lived where Coopers the wine shop is now, in a cottage that was pulled down.

'Jonathan Jeffcoat owned Jeffcoat Row, a row of cottages opposite this house. [These cottages were only pulled down in the late 1930s.] He was a professional photographer and took very good pictures of the church. He lived in what is now 3 St. Andrew's Road. My father was connected with the Jeffcoat people. Mr. Williams, who had a pork butcher's shop in Old High Street, worked with Tom Coster, and was a fellow who would go and kill a pig and sell it on the side so to speak, in what we would call a very rough shop for butchering. My mother bought the property and set up in business there.

'Before Horwood Close and the Shell Garage were built in London Road, the Rev. Blackburn used to live in a house, now demolished. Cecil Sharp was staying with them one holiday week-end, when the Morris dancers went to dance there. Cecil Sharp took down the dance tunes, set them to music, and after that the Morris dancers used to go and dance there once a year, in memory of that occasion. Bill Kimber was very much connected with Cecil Sharp. He played the concertina. Of course a lot of Quarry men will tell you that it was not Kimber who started the Morris dancing, but Mark Cox, the landlord of the Chequers, with Bill as one of his team. Mark Cox used to play the violin, and I have an old photograph of him doing so. Kimber was in the dancing team, but Cecil Sharp was the man who really put it on record. The tunes were recorded and set down to music, and that's when it really became something.

'Dr. Hitchings senior was the doctor when my father was living. We had to go to Holywell to get him but quite soon after that he had his house built where Fine Fare is now. That was in the early nineties. And young Dr. Hitchings, his son, lived there later. Before the First World War broke out he headed a petition to preserve Wootten's Park for Headington, and then the war came and the money was given back to the people who had subscribed.

'When we opened our outfitting shop in the London Road [closed in 1977] there was nothing on the corner [in 1920]. That was an open piece of ground. The next house, which is now the Trustees Savings Bank, belonged to a Mr. Griffin, and he had a petrol pump. On the other side there was Smith's shoe shop. Next door to us was a newsagent Mr. Hewitt. Then the next pair was put up: the right hand one was taken by Barclays Bank, and the other one by Mr. Arnold Vallis, who had a music shop. He was the son of the Headington Quarry baker. There was nothing else from there to Stephen Road. The place where Lloyds Bank is now was Mr. George Coppock's bungalow. He built the houses in Ramsay Road and also many in Old High Street and Manor Road. Next to that was Percy Griffin, the jeweller: he was Reg Griffin's brother. Next to that was the old lodge belonging to the Wootten estate, and a chap called Teddy Gomme used to live at the lodge. There was nothing between the Lodge and Sandy Lane, Osler Road as it is now. On the other side of the road on the corner of Windmill Road where the Quick Service Boot Shop is, was the Headington Post Office. Mr. and Mrs. Rudd used to keep that. The house where Eddie Hall lived belonged to the two Miss Mobbs, and next to them was Freddie Brown, who was a Post Office official. Then next to that lived Jim Berry, who was a postmaster. Then came Dr. McKay's house, and next door was an antique shop which later moved to Little Clarendon Street. Then came New Road, now called Kennet Road. Where Boots' new shop is now, Mr. Barson, a master builder, lived, and from there to New High Street was Mr. Hall's property. On the other side of Osler Road, where Manor Buildings are, there were two old cottages set back, with long gardens coming down to the road, and Mr. George Mattock lived in one of them. I believe he was the local tax collector. After that, along London Road, there was Mrs. Blackburn's where the Morris dancing took place, and further down was all allotments.

'The red brick development up Sandy Lane, now Osler Road, on the football side was part of the Manor estate. All Wootten's park from Cuckoo Lane in Old High Street to the London Road was bought by Kingerlees and sold off in plots. Houses were built very quickly after the First World War, almost before it had finished, and the builder got about £500 as a subsidy for putting them up, and sold them for round about £650.

'I remember Bury Knowle being opened as a public park by the Mayor of Oxford Mr. Brown, sometime in the thirties.

'The waits used to come at Christmas; Tolley was one, and Callaway, who was also a member of the Oxford Theatre orchestra. We used to love to hear them. We had mummers too: old Fred Loads, Jim Smith, Raspberry Louch. The White Hart was their headquarters. I remember the Foresters fête and the village band. It was in the yard of the Black Boy and we youngsters used to listen to the music.

'The Oddfellows' fête used to be held somewhere round by the Britannia. The band in each case would tour the village. Headington possessed a brass band and a drum and fife band at one time and a minstrel show was held in the British Workman. My husband was one of the minstrels.'

Mrs. Iris Masters

Another of the many people with long memories is Mrs. Iris Masters, who now lives at 33 Barton Lane. She is the daughter of Mrs. Mattock, one of the founder members of the Headington Women's Institute, and of William Mattock, brother of John Mattock the rose-grower, who was a florist and nurseryman at Blenheim Nurseries in Barton. Barton was then a little hamlet at the end of Barton Lane.

One of her earliest memories was when her grandmother took her down to see the bees, and told her that she should always tell the bees if she was ever in trouble. 'I have kept bees ever since, but I did miss telling them when my mother died, and I lost two hives.

'The village itself was very pretty. I've heard there was an old school up the Croft at the back of the Bell, where young gentlemen came before going to University. There used to a right of way there. Just before my time there was a very hard winter in 1881, and married men had 1s 6d a day and the single men 1/- a day. My grandmother, Mrs. John Mattock, made soup for them. The men were mostly builders, but they could not work because of the hard winter. They used to work with the Headington hard stone.

'Laurel Farm belonged to the Woottens of Headington House. They were a big family and Monty Wootten shot himself because he had become overdrawn at the Bank. I heard the shot. He was a partner of Wootten, Parsons and Thomson in the High Street, Oxford. When the family had gone, Headington House was empty for some years. I understand that years ago Mr. Franklin gave £1,000 for Headington House and park. The park, which went right to the main road, was sold for building plots at a very low price.

'I saw the first motor car go up the main road with a lady and gentleman going at what I thought was a high speed, but nothing compared with today. Along Barton Lane there were wheat fields where this house is now, and on the other side I was told by older men that corn grew. In 1917, fifteen elm trees blew down and the lane was blocked for six months before they could get them away.

'I went to an old dame school, Miss Steff's, just opposite the gates of the Rookery, and she used to tell us that on the opposite side of the road were the remains of a Saxon castle. It was a hunting lodge, and there definitely was, in my young days, a number of big stones about, and some part of the wall. Where the parish hall is now there used to be a little pond, where it had all fallen in. I do know there is an underground passage from the Rookery. You can still see the door at the Rookery, because I asked last time I was down

A group at Miss Steff's school in the twenties.

there, and it goes to the church. Captain Price's butler went down one day, and walked along it for a considerable distance until he found the air was too foul. Stoke Place is thought by a lot of people to be a private road, but it has always been a right of way to Elsfield. In my young days there was a path down one side and there were three old cottages at the bottom. A cobbler used to sit up on the wall, and you could hear him tapping at the shoes.

'Mr. E.J. Hall* put up all those houses in what we used to call Westbourne Terrace, where there are now shops on the left hand side of the main road. This was always called the Turnpike; some of the old people still do so. Those houses were built by a man who could neither read nor write. They cost him £50 each, and the men there worked at a very low wage. In 1918 some of them were sold for £150–£250. Mr. Hall, who owned the cinema, bought up a lot of property in Headington. When he bought White Lodge, the oak staircase was taken out and sold to some Americans.

'In St. Andrew's Road they pulled down the row of thatched cottages, and there was a road that went down by the side by the church. I can just remember houses being put up

---

*Mr. E.J. Hall owned a small tobacconist's shop in Cornmarket Street, Oxford. He became a City Councillor. He transformed Headington, building the cinema, a block of shops at the corner of New High Street and London Road, a squash court at the top of Old High Street, the Plaza Dance Hall on the site of the present MacMarket, etc.

down Stoke Place. Morris, the builder, did a lot of building and you can still pick out houses in Headington that he built. The deeds of the piece of land on the west side of Old High Street, owned by the Liddells, which Mrs. Ballachey gave and which Charlie Morris had, were lost. But that land was given for a parish room.

'I never saw anything but carts up the Croft. There were rights of way for coal carts, where they used to deliver coal to the cottages. Often on a Sunday the villagers used to net sparrows there. All the Croft paths were made of Headington hard, before they asphalted it.

'Headington and Quarry were the laundries for all the Oxford colleges. Bob Cross, who was gardener at the Grange, told me, how at the age of 11 he used to run behind Mr. Kerry's cart when they took the laundry back to the colleges. There were no lights on the roads then. There were three or four people who used to have laundries in St. Andrew's Road. Mrs. Cooper used to take it in the cottages, but it was mostly done at Quarry.

'We have always thought ourselves a bit superior to New Headington. They were very pretty girls at Quarry due to the fact that their ancestors came from Cornwall, out of the tin mines. They seemed to have unusual irises in their eyes. There was a man up there, Mr. Coppock, who used to be paid 10d every time he went to the Eye Hospital for examination, and they came to the conclusion that it was working down the mines that made the irises change. These Cornish folk came to build the colleges. They dug the stone and then they made themselves houses. So Quarry consisted mainly of stone masons.

'They had a feast out here in the field that the Priory has now, which belonged to the Black Boy. It was on Whit Monday. There was a man named Raspberry Louch, who drank pretty heavily, and there was a greasy pole and a leg of lamb or pork at the top, as a prize for the one who could get there. Raspberry Louch used to drink a lot of his mother's home-made wine, and then he would come along and streak up to the top and get the leg of lamb or pork. My mother thought it was far too rowdy for my sister and me to go there.

'There was Morris dancing in the street, and at Christmas there were mummers and handbell ringers. In the belfry you would find a man named Bennett who was a great ringer and the team leader for silver bells. Then there was little Billy Taylor's band, that used to play at Whitsun or Hospital Sunday. It was a drum and fife band, and I always call it little Billy Taylor. He was a church warden here for a number of years.

'We always had the flower show in Manor Park. That was a great day because they had poultry and dogs and flowers and races, and George Stace's father used to teach children the maypole. That went on right up to the end of the First World War, and after that everything completely changed. On August Bank Holiday they always decorated the village cross, tying it round with bay and yew, a bit of holly and ivy. We used to make a wreath and trail it round the cross. I've done it quite a number of times, and on May Day we used to go round the village and sing:

> A bunch of may I have brought you
> and at your door I stand,
> It is but a bit well spread about,
> the work of our Lord's hand.

> Good morning ladies and gentlemen
> I wish you a happy day,
> I've come to show my garland
> and 'tis the first of May.

'They used to have Fair Sunday at St. Giles' Fair, where they always ate blackberry and apple tart and lamb if they could afford it. You could then get a leg of lamb for about 3s 6d.

'My mother had a gentleman from India staying for a while, who was a friend of Colonel Hoole's at the Manor. Colonel Hoole had been in India. Mrs. Hoole was a very beautiful woman: a Rajah wanted to buy her. The two most beautiful women I have ever seen were Mrs. Hoole and Mrs. Wootten. They were very tall and they wore long Victorian sweeping frocks.

'Anyone could go down to Manor Farm and get a pint of skimmed milk for a half penny. The farm was a very different building from what it is now. From Dunstan Road to Marston there was a footpath across the fields. You could go along a green lane and get out into Marston, before the bypass was built.

'Just outside Headington House there were three Tudor doorways, the remains of almshouses. Then there were these long alleys, which we used to call The Hawthorn. The one that goes from Old High Street out into Osler Road, that was The Hawthorn. Where you crossed Osler Road to go down towards Oxford, was always known as Cuckoo Lane. The red squirrels used to be down there a lot when I was young.

'Old Mrs. Jacobs, who lived at Barton, was a carrier, and she brought the laundry from town and took it back. Albert Pratt did it after the First World War.

'Old Papa Wells, who lived at 29 Old High Street, drove the fly for people who wanted to go to Oxford. Then just before the First World War Mr. Dring ran a bus called the Rocket for sixpence return. My father used to go to market Wednesdays and Fridays and we came back up Headington Hill, which was much steeper than it is now. I used to drive the cart in the middle of the High Street, where there was hardly any traffic. Oxford really was a beautiful city in those days. They had horse trams later on. I walked to Oxford when I got older. I had to walk to the old Milham Ford School as most children did, and walk back again. There were only the Church schools then, no Council schools, and at Margaret Road, only fields.

'Opposite the Black Boy was an elm tree, and there was another tree opposite the side way to the church. The ordinary people went in by that gate, they did not go in by the main gate, as only gentry went through there. Their carriages used to stop so that the elderly people could get out and walk down the main path. The side walk was used a lot and people used to go round the church and in the back way.'

Mr. Jack Stow

Jack Stow, with whom we were privileged to talk a short while before he died in 1974, had more colourful memories. He will be widely known as the Secretary of the Headington Bowls Club since the Second World War.

He was born at the Bell public house in 1888 and went to Miss Steff's school in the little tin hut opposite the Parish Hall. 'After that I went up to the infants' school which was at the side of the Bury Knowle entrance, and this school was run by Mrs. Crozier and her two daughters. From there I went to the Field School in London Road, and then I went to the Wesleyan Higher Grade School which was down Bulwarks Alley, New Road, Oxford.

Talking of the houses in the village, he remembered the old cottage next to Miss Steff's tin hut school which in 1891 was occupied by Samson Smith. 'That was pulled down, and Dr. Massie's gardener lived in the new one in its place. In Old High Street there is the British Workman's Club, formed as a temperance club. Villagers could buy a jug of soup there for 2d. in the year 1898. The British Workman was run by trustees, of whom Mr. Bert Edney was one and William John Berry another.

'Headington Post Office was opposite the Black Boy and was run by Mrs. Rudd, who also sold groceries. Twopence was offered to anyone standing by the old elm tree to deliver the orders.

'A cab and fly business was run by Mr. Wells, whose premises were on the left of Old High Street, near to the London Road. He would go to the station and meet trains at any time and bring passengers back to Headington for 2s 6d. Berry the bakers would cook Sunday dinners for the sum of 3d. At weddings old Mr. Henry Cousens would exercise his prerogative of opening the carriage door for the bride to step out. He used to live down Church Lane. At the wedding of Johnnie Coppock who lived in the third cottage up from the Black Boy, the horses were taken out of the carriage, and it was man-pulled from the

The old Black Boy with its famous tree.

church, round the Vicarage and down Sandy Lane, and then round left to London Road and left again to Old High Street.

'Joseph Stringer was a farmer who ran Barton farm opposite the Prince's Castle, and often on Saturdays he would travel to the Golden Cross in Cornmarket Street, Oxford. His mare Polly used to take him in a little light cart, and on the journeys home Polly was in sole control if the farmer had had too many drinks. Polly would gallop all down High Street, Oxford, through St. Clements, up Headington Hill, turn left into Sandy Lane, negotiate the sharp turn at the Croft and the Vicarage, and finally stop at the farm gates in Barton Lane. The problem was then to get the farmer out of the cart. His son Sid and I solved it many times by fetching a bundle of straw, letting down the tailboard of the cart and tipping the farmer out onto it.

'In the old days Headington had to make its own amusement. There was the brass band, and the drum and fife band and in 1904 the minstrel group was formed. Performances were given in the British Workman and Field Schools.

'There was a Baptist chapel in the High Street, which had living accommodation overhead, next to two stone cottages. The small chapel and burial ground in the Croft, now in ruins, was still used. The city water was brought to Headington in approximately 1897 and the sewer pipes laid. They were very deep from Windmill Road and had to be tunnelled.

'In Old High Street there was a village smithy, worked by my uncle, Arthur Stow. He used to shoe the horses and do repairs. A little higher up from the smithy was a wheelwright and undertaker's shop, which was run by Mr. Sawyer. He made the wheels and repaired the farm wagons.

'Opposite the Priory was the old butcher's shop belonging to Harry Berry. There was also another butcher's shop just below that opened after Berry's—a small shop which sold sausages and a few things. Bill Wheeler took the shop that Mrs. Rudd used to run, which had been the Post Office. There was a small dairy farm in the Croft run by the Miss Wilkins and they used to have cows. (See p. 21) You could buy dairy produce from them.

'The Pound really did not belong to anybody, it was just an open piece of ground which is now walled in. If cattle strayed, or horses or sheep, they were put in there.

'Miss Clarke used to live in 10 St. Andrew's Road. She was a well-known church worker and played the organ in church. She also helped with the coal and clothing clubs, which were held in the British Workman. The villagers used to go up to the British Workman and pay a penny or whatever they could afford on the cards during the summer. Then at the end of the summer they could buy coal or clothes, according to how much money they had put on the cards.

'Mr. Wylie, who lived at the Grange after 1922, took an interest in forming the Headington Sports Group, which bought the fields where football is now played and the bowling green. Mr. Wylie was one of the directors and just after Mr. Wylie died in 1948 I became one of the directors of that company. Then we sold out the ground to the Headington Football Club. In 1970 the bowls ground was bought by the bowls club.

'As for thatched cottages in the village, there were three adjoining the British Workman, going up towards London Road, and they were pulled down as far back as I can remember. There were two stone thatched cottages in St. Andrew's Road, next to the little alley that leads up to the Croft. There were two or three old thatched cottages by the Black Boy and the ones owned by Mr. Bell at the Hermitage were thatched. Old Dick Mills was the local thatcher, and he lived in New Headington.'

Mrs. Coggins

Another invaluable source of information was Mrs. Coggins, née Webb, now living in the Croft. She has been in the village for over 75 years and her mother and father before her. 'Four generations of my family have been born here, that is myself, and my children and my grandchildren. My father was a cowman for Mr. John Wiggins at Manor Farm. I was the youngest of 15 and I have been here all my life. When I was married my parents did not want me to leave, so my husband and I had half this house.

'In the Croft there were two thatched cottages by the Bell, which were burnt down. Otherwise the Croft is just the same, except for the garages and sheds.

'The small chapel in the Croft was used when I was a little girl, and we were allowed to go there until we were 7 years old and then we had to transfer to the bigger chapel in Old High Street.

'In my twenties, the Post Office and general store on the corner of Old High Street was run by Mr. Rudd and his mother. Then they built the Post Office by the traffic lights in London Road which was then called the Turnpike. That's where they had the old turnstile, and father said it cost a penny to go through with a wagon and horse.

'Mr. Stow the blacksmith had a lovely old blacksmith's yard (51 Old High Street) just opposite the Hawthorn in Old High Street. We often stood there when we were girls and watched the horses being shoed. I was always so afraid they were going to hurt the horses' feet, because as children you don't realise that there is a proper way of putting on these things. Mr. Stow lived at the corner house by North Place.

'Then there was Bill Wheeler who later took Mrs. Rudd's corner shop. He lived with his mother in one of the cottages down Stoke Place. That's where we went for eggs.

'There was a row of cottages between the Priory and the Black Boy and then they were pulled down and the two houses that are there now were built [in 1909]. I think the new Black Boy was built because of widening the road at the corner, to go into Barton Lane. There was a big old tree there, and it was taken down before the new Black Boy was built. There was another big tree in St. Andrew's Lane, but someone set fire to that and burnt it down, as was done to Pullens Tree (in 1909) at the top of Headington Hill where there is a plaque.

'I went to the Field School in London Road, where Mr. Stace senior was the Headmaster. Mrs. Bridgewater, who was very strict, was headmistress for the girls because it was not a mixed school. It had boys on one side and girls on the other.

'On the Headington House side of Old High Street was all fields, where Mr. Montague Wootten kept his Jersey cows. There were two sons and two daughters in the Wootten family, and their cowman and other workmen lived in Laurel Farm, and the Court. I always said he gave his workmen some nice houses.

'As girls we often went up to watch the garden parties at White Lodge, with all their pretty dresses and big picture hats. It was something to look forward to, when you knew that Mr. Wootten was having a garden party. But you had to keep out of the way of the carriages and pairs that were going in.

'In the mornings before going to school, we went to fetch the milk from Manor Farm where my father worked for Mr. John Wiggins. That was before milk was delivered, and I know today they say it was not the right thing to do, but it never hurt people in days gone by.'

Miss Gertie Hedges, Miss Sylvia Parker and Mrs. Edie Dickinson

Next we had a splendid trio of Miss Gertie Hedges, Miss Sylvia Parker, and Mrs. Edie Dickinson, and though some of the information was lost on the tape because they were inclined to speak at the same time, much of interest was learnt. We started by asking Gertie Hedges who lived in the Rookery Cottages at the top of Stoke Place where she was

St. Andrew's Road when the old Black Boy existed.

born. 'Well', she said, 'there was a Mrs. Soames, and Dick Taylor, and Mrs. Phipps, they were all there. And Charlie Morris the builder [1 Stoke Place], and Miss Steff's school. That was a little private school and she used to charge 6d. an hour teaching us music. Then we moved and went into the little cottage opposite the church [16 St. Andrew's Road]. In the corner house was Mr. Somersford, the bank manager.' Later Gertie Hedges lived in St. Andrew's Lane.

Mrs. Dickinson was in the Black Boy when street lighting was first put in by the City in the twenties. Before that she paid rates to Bullingdon. She was in the Croft in 1909 when Mr. Montague Wootten shot himself, and Bill Wheeler came running round from the Post Office. When Wootten's ground was sold for £10 a plot her father could have 'kicked himself 50 times over because he was just too late to get one'.

One of the first people to have a motor car was Mr. Dockray from Stoke House, and Mr. Stowe, the veterinary surgeon at West Lodge. [Not to be confused with Mr. Stow, the blacksmith.] There were three cottages along the wall by West Lodge, where Mrs. Coppock, Tom Gammon, Florrie Brown, and old Mrs. Mabel Parker lived. The girls used to work as servants or maids in the houses. Mr. Aston the sweep lived in the little red-brick cottage which is now the Juel-Jensens' garage. Miss Shelford, who was something to do with the school board, lived in Monckton Cottage, now belonging to the Juel-Jensens, and when she moved over the street, to No. 81, she named that one Monckton Cottage as well, so there were two in the street. Mr. Stow the blacksmith was at the forge and Mr. Morris the builder did some thatching. Mr. Creese, known as 'Whistler Creese' because he was always whistling, lived at the British Workman. He imitated bird song very beautifully, and in this way trapped wild birds to sell. He used to do some chopping for Mrs. Chaundy, who owned the cottages.

Mrs. Dickinson went on 'I can always remember the cricket up at Mattock's nurseries, in that little field in Barton Road. And there was not much traffic in London Road, only the post. Reg [her husband] got run over by that. Dr. Hitchings lived in Windmill Road at first and he had a daughter. She lived for a long time in the house opposite us in Ash Grove, bought for her by Dr. Hitchings. He had a surgery in Kennet Road, attached to the side of the house, and he visited with a buggy and a horse, though he very often walked in a tail coat.'

Miss Sylvia Parker, who was born in the Croft in 1899, had some interesting memories. Her grandfather was Samson Smith who lived on the Bank opposite the Parish Hall where the present 39 St. Andrew's Road stands. 'He was a market gardener on the grounds to the west of Windmill Road, and Ernie, one of his sons, delivered the produce all over the place in a horse and cart.' Jack Berry also remembers Ernie Smith as quite a character, who owned a donkey called Edward and a Scottish terrier dog. Edward pulled a little cart loaded with vegetables which Ernie grew on a patch of the glebe land (church property in Old Road), and the terrier often rode on the donkey's back. Ernie was a great fisherman and often brought fish to Jack's father, Harry Berry, to be weighed—if they were specimens—or for him to eat as he was very fond of fresh water fish and eels. After Ernie's death, Edward the donkey went to Lower Farm to end his days in comfort. Miss Parker goes on: 'My grandfather was a very keen Baptist, and had 5 daughters and 4 sons, and lived till he was over 80. My father was a stone-waller and stone-mason, a builder really. He built the white flat-topped house in Osler Road, where the Sanctuaries lived. There were not many colleges he had not worked on.'

'The Turnpike was right across the top of Old High Street. If the farmers bringing cattle across would not pay, the cattle were put in the Pound. There used to be a big tree at the top of St. Andrew's Lane.

'There used to be several shops that have now gone—after all we only had the Co-op on the London Road. Warrens sold wet fish in the little cottage in Old High Street, No 86. And a fish cart came round every Monday. I remember the liquorice at Harold Rudd's.'

Miss Maggie Taylor

No local history could be considered complete without bringing in Maggie Taylor, sister of Dick Taylor, who for so many years was verger at the church. Miss Taylor is now living at Abbeyfield House in Stephen Road. She came to live in 1893 in one of the ten old thatched cottages in St. Andrew's Road, then Church Street, when she was three months old. Her grandmother, Mrs. Edel, lived in the cottage nearest to the Vicarage. She and her parents were next door but one. 'There were no houses opposite us in the grounds of Laurel Farm, and the present sheds were where the cows were kept. Mr. Ayres was Montague Wootten's cowman living in Laurel Farm about 1900.

'An aunt of Lord Olivier used to live in the house next to Berry's shop, 3 St. Andrew's Road, and she was a sister of Lady Nicholson, Sir Charles Nicholson's first wife, who lived in Church House. Before that the house was occupied by a Mrs. Chillman who kept it as a boarding house. When I came here, the Vicar was the Rev. Scott Tucker, and the Rev. R.W. Townson followed him. He introduced the 'High Church' tradition here. His brother was a curate here during some of the time the Rev. Scott Tucker was Vicar.

'When our old cottages in St. Andrew's Road came to an end in 1938 the stones from the floors were used for the path in the churchyard. And in Church Lane, now St. Andrew's Lane, Mrs. Tempero kept a lollipop shop, opening it only on Sundays. Opposite the old Vicarage was the Somersfords' house, and I lived in with the first Mrs. Somersford, and was paid 2/- a week wages. That was my first job—I worked from 6 o'clock in the morning till 10 o'clock at night. I did everything, cook as well as clean. Mother died in 1924 and I started doing the laundry, taking over from her in 1922, because she was ill for two years.

'For entertainment we had the flower show on August Bank Holiday in Colonel Hoole's park, which is now the John Radcliffe Hospital grounds. On Whit Monday we had the Oddfellows dinner with roundabouts and swinging boats in the field near where the Britannia is. I went to dances nearly every Saturday at the schools, paying 6d., and the M.C. for those dances was Mr. Bateman, and later Mr. Webb. We danced the waltz and the polka and the lancers and the valeta.

'Miss Davenport from London Road used to come to St. Andrew's Church in one of those old-fashioned carriages where the coachman sat behind and the lady in front—not a closed-in carriage. And during the church service the coachman had to walk the horses up and down outside. Mrs. Wootten was the last person to be buried in the churchyard, in the early 1900s. The old Baptist chapel was in the Croft. It did not hold many people, but the population was very different from what it is now. There was only one house in Windmill Road, with the Windmill cottages, up at the top. There were no houses on the London Road, only Westbourne Terrace, the red brick houses between the corner electric shop, and Bury Knowle Park. The police sergeant lived in the first house.

'The Relieving Officer, Mr. Butler, used to come from Cowley Road, when the parish relief was 3s 4d a week. My grandmother, Mrs. Edel, had it. Out of 3s 4d a week she used to pay 1s 3d a week rent for her cottage, and she had 2s 1d a week to live on. Mother used to give her her Sunday dinner, and she went to the Vicarage at one o'clock with a basin and a plate to cover it, and a two-pound stone jam jar. That was filled with dripping for her, and her vegetables were put in the basin and a piece of batter pudding, and the Vicar cut her slices of beef from the dining room table. And on top, on the plate, was put a jam turnover, to cut into three nice pieces for us children.

'Where Ash Grove and Chestnut Avenue are now [they were built in the late twenties] was Mr. Mattock's rose garden. He was Mrs. Masters' father. On the other side of the road were the fields, farmed from Mathers Farm.'

Mr. Bill Berry and Mr. Ken Berry

Now let us see what the Berry brothers can add to our local information. Their grandfather and grandmother, who came from the Islip area, had 12 children and came to live at Mathers Farm. The grandfather died when he was 54 (in 1888) but Grandma Berry brought up the family of 12 children and lived until she was 83 (1926). They moved from Mathers Farm to the present bakery during the First World War. It was built by A.E. Vallis (Nokey). Their father, Mr. W.J. Berry, ran the baking business, and their Uncle Harry, after serving his apprenticeship in Witney, took over the butchery business with a shop in Old High Street in 1908.

Mr. Bill Berry says 'I first remember the Bonds in the Black Boy. Edward was about two years older than I was. He taught me to ride a bicycle along Barton Lane—an ideal place to learn to ride a bicycle in those days—there was very little traffic and when you wanted to fall off, you fell on the bank on the right hand side. The pub was then in front of the present Black Boy, and they built the new one before they pulled the old one down. It was a very square corner but a very safe one, because you could not possibly go round at more than about ten miles an hour. The old Black Boy was a stone house, and they had the shute down to the cellar just by the Barton Lane corner, under the window. There used to be two mounting stones outside.

'I, like many others, first went to Miss Steff's private school, a kind of kindergarten, which had about 25 children and one teacher. Then I went to St. Andrew's School—all the Berry family went there. I must have started school when we were living at Mathers Farm, which was the family house. My Granny Berry lived there and father and mother

Mrs. Berry with her twelve children.

continued to live there until I was six. Then father had to buy or build something, because he got very short notice from the Bursar of Magdalen to vacate the farm. He nearly built a double-fronted shop and bakery in the Windmill Road. But Miss Huntingdon, who lived in the present bakery, said "I hear you have got to buy other premises, and my lease has only got two years to run. If the owner would sell it to you, I would let you have it sooner and you could build a bakery in the garden." And that is what happened. Father came to terms and bought the place and built the bakery. The first bakery was in Mathers Farm. The present kitchen of Mathers Farm was the shop and the rear door of the farm in Larkins Lane was the shop door. Father ran the baking business and Uncle Harry the butchery business. Before that Grandmother Berry used to run the farm and the butchery business and the bakery business. Grandfather Berry died when my father was fourteen, and father was the eldest of twelve. Grandma did not marry till she was about 35 and she had twelve children.

'I can remember delivering bread at the Rookery in Dr. Massie's time. There were possibly eight or nine staff in the house and ten or eleven in the garden and Dick Berry's father-in-law, Jack Crawford, who ran the little farm. We had to go down the lane and walk up to the house to deliver the bread. One Saturday evening, it was all very quiet. As I came away from the house I took a short cut up to the front gate pushing the two-wheeled truck we used in the village. It was about 7 o'clock, as we rarely finished until about that time. I was within 20 yards of the front gate when in walked Dr. Massie with his stick. He stood and looked at me and said "Good evening, baker. Are you not aware that the back entrance is for the use of tradesmen? I shall be glad if you will kindly remember that in future" and I crept out of the gate, saying "Thank you Sir".

'We used to deliver all round with a horse-drawn cart. On three days we shut the horse out while we had our meal and then started off again. On the other three days we stopped and had sandwiches.

'I remember the end of our delivery round used to be up the London Road where Major Fanshawe lived at Forest Lodge, where Nielsens are. On the way there we used to stop at a spot where the new church has been built in Collingwood Road—there were four farm cottages about a third of a mile from there. We used to pack about 8, 10, or possibly 12 loaves and a couple of bags of flour and carry them on our shoulders across to the cottages, while the other person went on with the horse and van to Forest Lodge to deliver. There were no street lamps or anything—it was absolutely pitch black. We had to stop there sometimes and put studs in the horse's shoes, if it was very frosty or icy. And talking of horses, the Beaufoys at Bury Knowle were keen hunting people and often three or four horses of theirs could be seen coming down Old High Street.

'Father was a councillor before he became sheriff in 1941. It was some time before that that they had quite a fight to get Bury Knowle Park kept as an open space for the community.'

Mr. Ken Berry remembers 'Bob Cross, who was 100 years old when he died in 1973. He likened his life span to a holly tree planted by his father some 100 years ago in the grounds of Townsend House, an Old People's Home at Bayswater where he died. Most of his life was spent as a gardener at the Grange in Larkins Lane, now the home of the Elliot-Smith family. And the garden was a show piece. It was always said he could not grow weeds. The occupant of the Grange at that time was a Miss Boss, a dignified lady who used to drive out in her carriage (see p. 28).

'Forty or fifty years ago there was a very much younger population in Old Headington with probably 35 young children in Church Lane and Church Street (now St. Andrew's Lane and Road). There were probably 20 or more belonging to families in Jeffcoat Row. Jeffcoat Row, demolished in the late thirties, used to run from Church Lane, across what is now part of Bill Berry's garden [1 Larkins Lane] and there was a communal gateway and paths leading off across the garden by the cottages. The farm, which is now William Orchard Close, was occupied by the Stopps family. They had a small dairy farm, which belonged to Mr. Wylie, then at the Grange, and they used to retail milk round Headington. Mrs. Tempero, who lived in 2 St. Andrew's Lane, persuaded Mr. Wylie to build her a bay window in her cottage, where she could have a lollipop shop. There was always a black cat asleep on the sweets in the lollipop window. But the sweets were jolly good.

'The parents of most of the children were farm or builders' labourers.

'After the 1914–1918 war, Albert Pratt, demobilised from the Army, started a carriage business, with a horse and trolley. He made two journeys to Oxford daily. Later the horse and trolley were replaced with a solid-tyred Ford pickup lorry, and he also did haulage work, from the cottage at the bottom of Larkins Lane.

'Then there was the annual Meet of the South Oxfordshire Foxhounds outside the White Hart. They usually found in Marston copse, now Copse Lane. And hand bell ringers, at which the Wiggins family were expert, usually came round on Boxing Day. The Wiggins family were also expert rick thatchers. One of them lived in Jeffcoat Row, and another, Cyril, in Barton Village.

'Old Mr. Hathaway, whose son now lives in Old High Street, used to farm the fields where the Northway estate now is. He also had the old farm buildings in Old High Street, which were reached from Headington House by the two small bridges. His house and yard were in Lime Walk. During the Second World War he used to collect milk from Mathers Farm where Mr. Jim Wheeler had built quite a reputation with his dairy shorthorn cows. (See Farms and Farming.) At Mathers Farm another event was the arrival of the threshing machine which took a day or two to set up. The local children loved watching it in the big barn that has now been converted into a house. It was in its way quite as impressive as the steam railway engine in the same decade. Most of the corn it threshed was grown in the field on the right of Barton Lane, now Chestnut Avenue, Ash Grove and Hawthorn Avenue. I can remember that as an open field, usually arable. Some of the corn was grown on Wick Farm, which Jim Wheeler was also farming at that time.

'Bareacres was put up in the twenties before Chestnut Avenue was built, as were the other houses in Barton Lane. The council houses on the main London Road were built years before, when Headington was a Rural District Council; then came the development in Barton Road, and after that the fields behind it were built on. Headington went into the City in 1929.

'In Larkins Lane, the cottage where Bill is now (1 Larkins Lane) was once part of the estate which belonged to the Grange. I remember a family named Morris living there, and next to them was the Phillips family. In the third lived a Miss Pratt, sister to Albert Pratt of the carriage business. Then the Edwards family came and they started a haulage business from the cottage at the bottom of Larkins Lane. The Stopps family carried on Church Hill farm for a time, and then the younger son took the Bell public house after Jack Williams. It was then just a beer house.

'I remember 76 Old High Street as a greengrocer's shop, run by Mrs. Somerville, whose husband had a small market garden next to Bury Knowle Park, where the car park is now. In 1936 Dick Brown moved in with his family [until 1960]. His sister, Florrie Brown lives at 2 St. Andrew's Lane. Their father was working for Jim Wheeler when he farmed at Wick Farm. He was a well-known gardener, and they lived at Cemetery Cottage for a long time.

'The annual village fête and flower show was held in Manor Park on August Bank Holiday. Everybody went to it, including the local band, and there was a good programme of sports, with bowling for a pig as an attraction. That was in the time of Colonel Hoole. It was always said that the four lime trees along Old High Street by the Priory belonged to the Lord of the Manor.

'Headington had a very flourishing cricket club at the turn of the century. My father said he took part in the winning of the Airey Cup in 1900. They had a first class team. But between then and the beginning of the 1914 war, it fell away and ceased to exist. It was not really revived until the land now occupied by the Oxford United Football Club came into the market and about a dozen public-spirited people subscribed the money to buy this land to provide opportunities for amateur sport. This was to include football, cricket, tennis and bowls. This worked out quite well for a few years. Then the football club flourished, the tennis club fell away, and the cricket club allowed itself to be pushed out of the ground. Mr. Horace Bradley, then living at Barton End, gave the ground in Barton Road, which is now the headquarters of the cricket club. Barton End reminds me of the first occupant, who was Major Rowell. Then it was occupied by the M.P. for Oxfordshire, Mr. Gifford Fox. After him came Mr. Horace Bradley, (d. 1945) and then it became an Old People's Home.

'Coming to the church, my father used to say that Mr. Townson's High Church ideas were not acceptable to many of the congregation and father and many of the members of

Headington United Cricket XI, 1900.

the choir left and went to Highfield Church. Alan Edney, with his father Bert Edney, his uncle Will Edney and my father, William Berry, sang at All Saints for many years but some of us stayed at St. Andrew's as choirmen—Jack and Dick Berry and I, and Ralph and Arthur Cattle. At St. Andrew's we had a choir of about 14 boys and 8 men. We were paid ½d per service. At the end of a quarter we had got about 1s 10½d. The eleven o'clock Eucharist was fairly well attended and we had 80 to 90 people regularly at the evening service. The organist in those days was George Stace, Headmaster of the local school and a great musician and choirmaster. His favourite hymn was "Lead, Kindly Light", the harmony of which he said was wonderful.

In 1888 my grandfather was one of the first to be buried in the cemetery in Dunstan Road. I can remember the cemetery house being occupied by Tom White who then farmed the land where the hospital is now. Then came Percy Sumner, the cemetery superintendent. I remember Arthur Sanctuary, the administrator of the hospital, saying about 45 years ago that it would be the site of one of the main hospitals in the country. It was about the time that Sunnyside and the Osler Pavilion were built. Sunnyside was the specialist home for consumptive cases and Dr. Stobie was the consultant.

'I can remember Army manoeuvres taking place on that land. There was a great camp of cavalry there in the First World War, with about 1,000 troops. I think Tom White supplied some of the food for the horses.'

Professor E.G.T. Liddell and Mrs. Liddell

And then listening to Professor and Mrs. Liddell of the Hermitage, to Mrs. Horscroft, who used to live in one of the Headington House lodges, and to Mrs. Corby, whose husband once had a tobacconist's shop near the Headington crossroads, we hear the following accounts.

Mrs. Liddell had talked with Miss Levett, then over 100, [she died in 1975 aged 101] but having clear memories of when she had come to Old Headington with her family in 1890. She went as an apprentice teacher at St. Andrew's School, and when qualified to Margaret Road School. Her brother bought Jesmond Cottage in Old High Street, but did not live in it. He also bought the Close and lived there until he sold it to Professor Douglas, Professor of Geology at the University. Later he lived in 81 Old High Street. There were many craftsmen in Old High Street, and a Mr. Williams, a pork butcher, lived at 76 Old High Street next to Miss Levett's home. No 77 was a 'keyhole house', and when old Mr. Godfrey procured the key on the death of the owner, he became the new owner of the house.

Professor Liddell recalled the first motor buses in 1912 or 1913. That was when William Morris was putting buses on the road in competition with horse trams. You had to buy a ticket for them from an agent on the route, as they were not licensed as public vehicles. The trams only came to the foot of Headington Hill. From there you had to take a charabanc or horse coach which left the foot of Headington Hill two or three times a day, and came up to Dring's stables just about where the traffic lights are now. Going the other way, from the bottom of Headington Hill you took the horse tram into central Oxford. The

Cottage at the corner of Sandy Lane (now Osler Road) and London Road.

horse buses used to go up the Woodstock Road to Wolvercote. They changed the horses at the Horse and Jockey which is opposite Bevington Road. They did two or three journeys and then changed horses.

The Liddells rented the Hermitage in 1924 and 18 months later they bought it from Mr. Bell. They have made no alterations to the house, but they remember hearing that Mr. Bell pulled down two cottages next door because he did not like having neighbours too close. That is now part of their garden (see p. 33).

About 1927, the Urban District Council put up the lamps and improved the side walks. But there was a bit of fuss because the City took up some Headington hard kerbing and began to use it to mend the wall on the main road, near Morrell Bridge. Dr. John Johnson, of Bareacres, objected and managed to stop it.

The Liddells bought their small plot of garden opposite the Hermitage from Charlie Morris the builder. He told them that the price of land in Headington was £3 per foot for frontage. Mrs. Masters tells us that this plot was given by Mrs. Ballachey for a parish room.

Mrs. Horscroft

Mrs. Horscroft used to live on the London Road in South Lodge which belonged to Headington House. It was just about where the wine shop (No 79) and Ideas (No 79c) are now. Her family moved into it in 1914, when there was nothing else on the London Road.

'It was quite a big bungalow with four very large rooms and a nice large kitchen. You had to go down steps from the kitchen into a paved yard, with four sheds on the other side. My grandmother bought another piece of land to make it square,' Mrs. Horscroft tells us. There was a stone wall round the front, right up to Osler Road. Dr. Hitchings' house was on the opposite side of the London Road. The Wootten estate was then being carved up into building plots. In front of the Horscroft bungalow there were four lime trees, with the drive at the side going up to Headington House, part of which was the garden for the bungalow. Between 1918 and 1930 many more houses were built, Griffins the jewellers, Bowermans the butchers, and Aldis on the corner. At the opposite corner of Osler Road there was only one house until the shops were built in the 1930s. Mrs. Horscroft's parents bought the bungalow for £450 and sold it again for £1,000 after four years, to Kings, the motor people. The new owners took it down and reconstructed it just as it was on Boars Hill for their gardener.

Mrs. Horscroft remembered the allotments on the south side of London Road, as far as Stile Road, and beyond the school as far as the Laurels (the old workhouse). Mr. Hall wanted to build a cinema next to the bungalow, but the Council turned it down and it had to be built, in the twenties, away from the main road. That was the beginning of the Moulin Rouge in New High Street.

Stephen Road was built up in the late twenties. The main road by then had been made up, but when Mrs. Horscroft was a girl there was no street lighting. She used to be very frightened to walk along the road in the dark, so her grandmother often used to meet her when she returned from Oxford where she worked as a clerk at the Post Office, paying $2\frac{1}{2}$d to go to Carfax on one of William Morris's buses. The street lights were put in about 1924. Cuckoo Lane beyond Osler Road was called the Oxford Fields, and the path through the Wootten's estate was the Hawthorn. At the end of Osler Road, where now there are shops and the doctors' surgery, was one double-fronted house, owned by a Mr. Mattock, who used to stand at the gate, watching everyone go by.

Mrs. Corby

Mrs. Corby came from Somerset in 1912 to the old school house at Bury Knowle Park entrance [3 North Place]. Her husband was an outfitter at Shepherd and Woodward. At that time the 4 houses in Old High Street with gardens parallel to North Place belonged to the Corby family. They were open at the back into Bury Knowle Park, then occupied by the Laing family who had horses and gave big parties in the grounds.

Mrs. Corby's children went in about 1917 to Miss Steff's school, when she was an elderly lady but still teaching in the old tin hut down by Ruskin Hall. Mrs. Corby did much voluntary work and was the first person to take round National Savings stamps for sale in Headington and Barton. She housed many evacuees, during the Second World War, when her husband was an air raid warden. Later he had a tobacconist's shop at the top of Old High Street.

Miss Katharine Woods

In 1915 when Miss Woods arrived in Headington, she tells us that there were very few buildings between there and Forest Hill, apart from Barton village street. Only three houses stood on the north side of the London Road apart from the little stone lodge, and although the top of Old High Street (in the Wootten's park) was divided into building plots, nothing had yet been built. There were a few shops in London Road—Smith's the shoe shop, a chemist and one other. Opposite was Dr. Hitchings' house with a delightful garden and a few small houses between him and the crossroad, in one of which the Woods first lived. There was a wheelwright's shop next to the Royal Oak, and the wood was sawn up where the present bowling green is. It was just a sand pit and there was so much subsidence that it was not safe for building. There is still half of a semi-detached pair in Osler Road, because it was found unsafe to build the second half. (See also Schools).

Stone walls in the Croft.